CYPRIOTE ART

IN THE BRITISH MUSEUM

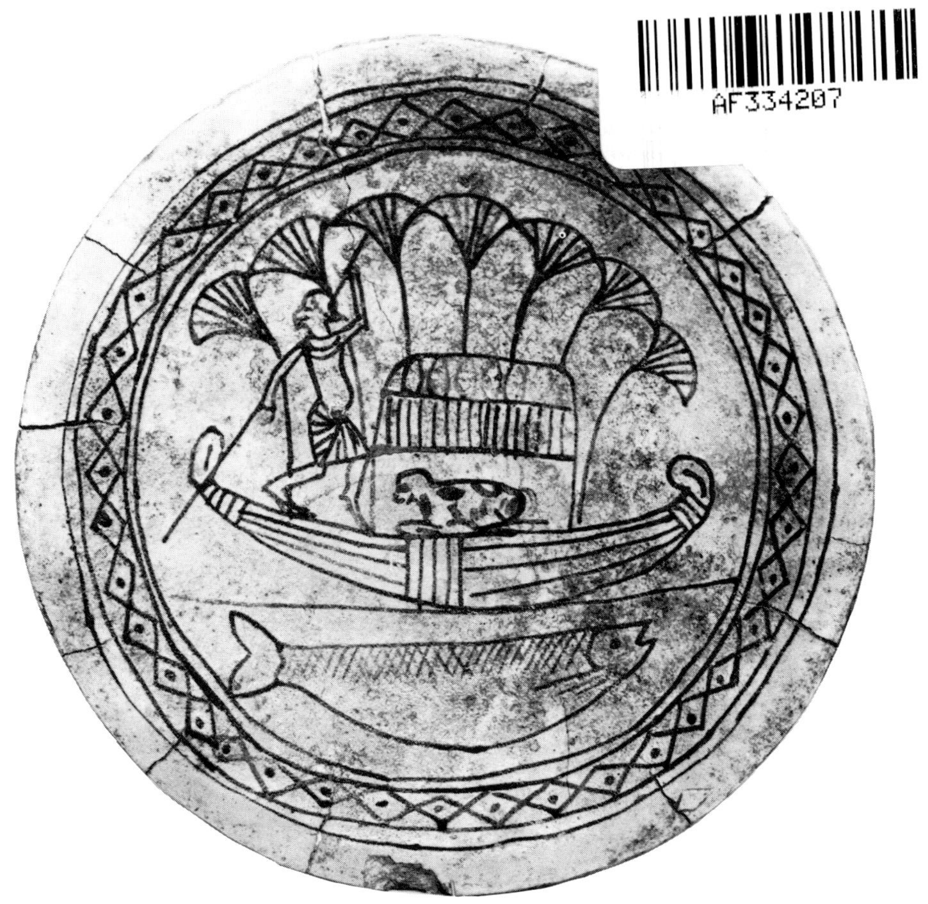

Edited by B. F. Cook

Published for the Trustees of the British Museum by
British Museum Publications Limited

Published by British Museum Publications Limited,
6 Bedford Square, London, WC1B 3RA

Designed by Paul Sharp

ISBN 0 7141 1268 2

Set in 11pt Monophoto Garamond by Filmtype Services Limited, Scarborough
Printed and bound in Great Britain by William Clowes (Beccles) Limited
Beccles and London

Front cover: Terracotta horseman, from Amathus.
700–600 BC. *BMC Terracottas* A 166. H.12.0 cm.

Title page: Faience bowl of Egyptian type from Enkomi.
1897.4–1.1042. D.22.7 cm.

Inside front cover: Limestone male statue, Neo-Cypriote
style, from Tamassos. 600–550 BC. *BMC Sculpture* C 68.
H.145.0 cm.

Inside back cover: Terracotta head, Proto-Cypriote
style, from Tamassos. 660–600 BC. 1910.6–20.1.
H.36.0 cm.

Coins reproduced actual size except where indicated

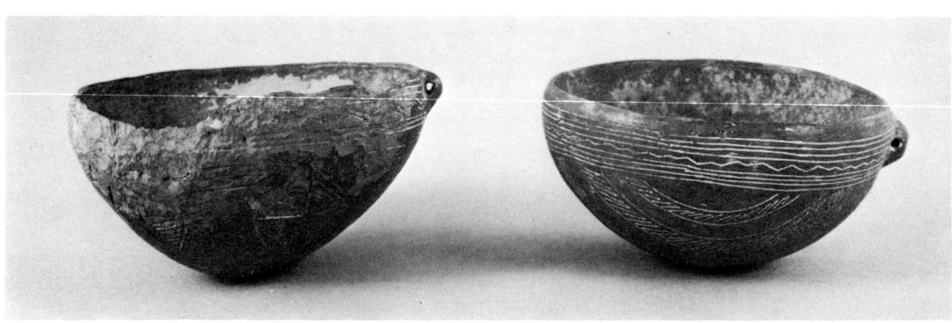

Red Polished ware bowls, with incised decoration. *BMC Vases* a) C62. H.6.4 cm, D.11.7 cm;
b) C61. H.5.7 cm, D.11.4 cm.

Contents

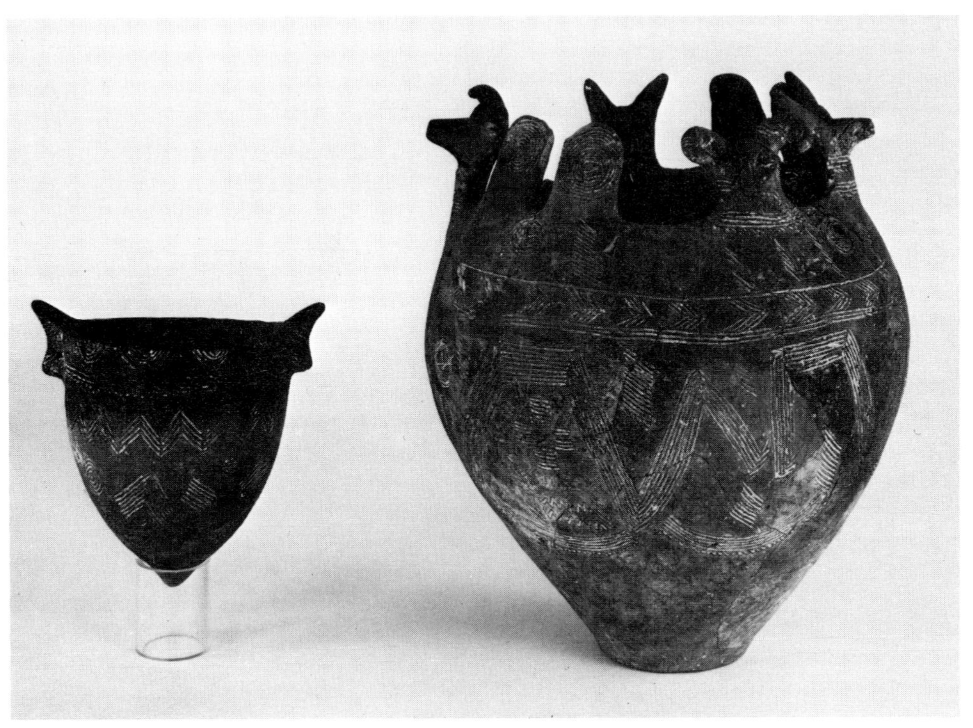

Ear-lug pot and cult-vessel of the Early Cypriote I Period, from Vounous Tomb 105.
a) 1939.12–17.11. H.14.0 cm; b) 1939.2–17.13. H.28.0 cm.

PREFACE

The British Museum is fortunate in possessing one of the largest collections of Cypriote antiquities outside of Cyprus itself. This collection was mainly acquired during the nineteenth century, at first by purchase and later by excavation.

The first Cypriote material to enter the collection was a group of eight stone sculptures, twenty terracottas and an inscription, bought in 1852 from Henry Christy, who had collected them at Larnaca. Twenty years later the Museum bought a larger collection of stone sculptures that had been excavated in the sanctuary of Apollo at Idalion by Sir Robert Hamilton Lang. The first important gift consisted of over three hundred terracottas, presented by D. E. Colnaghi in 1866.

In 1876 over a hundred items of pottery, stone, bronze and terracotta were bought from General Luigi Palma di Cesnola, who had dug extensively in Cyprus during his term as American Consul on the island. The larger part of his collection had already been acquired by The Metropolitan Museum of Art in New York. Unfortunately the objects that the British Museum bought from Cesnola have no individual provenances.

During the last two decades of the nineteenth century, large numbers of antiquities were acquired from official excavations in Cyprus. M. Ohnefalsch-Richter's excavation in the sanctuary of Artemis at Achna, east of Idalion, provided stone sculptures and terracottas in 1882, while antiquities acquired from the same excavator in 1884 included pottery of the Early and Middle Bronze Age from Phoinikias and Hellenistic material from Salamis. More material came from Salamis in 1890, excavated by H. A. Tubbs and J. A. R. Munro and presented to the Museum by the Cyprus Exploration Fund. This was followed by Classical and Hellenistic material from their excavations at Marion.

From 1894 the British Museum itself conducted a series of excavations financed by the bequest of Miss E. T. Turner. Cemeteries excavated at Amathus in 1893–94, at Kourion in 1895 and at Enkomi in 1896 yielded large quantities of Bronze-Age and later pottery of both Cypriote and Mycenaean types, as well as contemporary objects of stone, terracotta and bronze. By agreement, one third of the finds from these excavations were deposited in the Cyprus Museum, the remainder being brought to London. In all cases the tomb-groups were kept together.

Further excavations of Bronze-Age cemeteries at Maroni and Hala Sultan Tekke in 1897–98 produced terracottas, ivories and jewellery as well as quantities of pottery. In 1899 the finds at Klavdhia were mainly from the Late Bronze Age, while a smaller excavation at Kouklia yielded some material from the Iron Age as well as from the Late Bronze Age.

It is hardly possible that a collection built up this way should be wholly representative of the range of Cypriote antiquities. Remains of the Neolithic and Chalcolithic periods have only been discovered in Cyprus in recent years, and the fortunes of earlier excavations left the British Museum with little material from the very end of the Bronze Age or the beginning of the Geometric period, and with no Cypriote examples of mosaics or wall-paintings from later times.

Some of these gaps will now never be filled. The need to retain in Cyprus itself the most important examples of the archaeological inheritance of the island means that the Roman mosaics, for example, cannot be made available to museums elsewhere. At the same time, through the generosity of the Government of the Republic of Cyprus and the far-sighted policy of its Department of Antiquities, it is possible to participate in official excavations and so obtain from them some of the less important material that nonetheless has considerable archaeological interest. The British Museum, for example, has already acquired some representative fragments of Chalcolithic pottery for the Department of Prehistoric and Romano-British Antiquities, and it is planned to continue this mutually beneficial collaboration between the British Museum and the Department of Antiquities in Cyprus.

It is regrettable that there has been no permanent exhibition of Cypriote antiquities in the British Museum for many years. The rearrangement of the upper galleries of the Department of Greek and Roman Antiquities will provide an opportunity to remedy this unfortunate situation. In the meantime the various sections of this book, each written by a scholar with a particular interest in the relevant period, are intended both to indicate the scope of the British Museum's collections from Cyprus and to serve as an introduction to Cypriote antiquities in general.

B. F. COOK
Keeper of Greek and Roman Antiquities

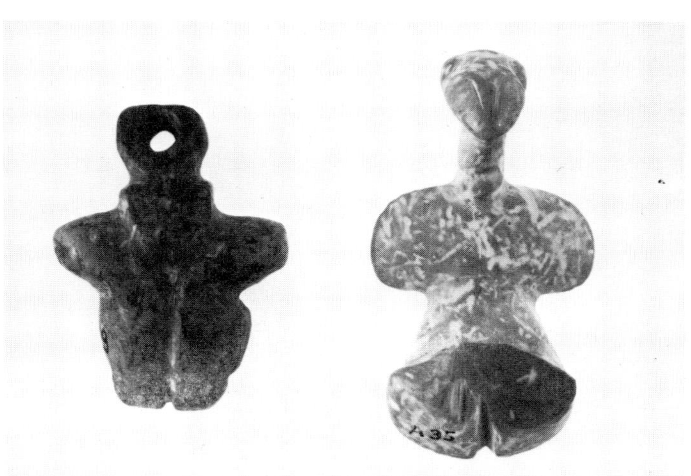

Chalcolithic stone figurines from Klavdhia and Maroni. a) 1899.12–29.41. H.2.9 cm; b) 1898.12–1.55. H.3.8 cm.

Chronological Table

The absolute dates are approximate

Neolithic, *Khirokitia* culture		7000–6000 BC
Neolithic, *Sotira* culture		4500–3750 BC
Chalcolithic		3500–2500/2300 BC
Early Bronze Age	I	2300–2075 BC
	II	2075–2000 BC
	III	2000–1900 BC
Middle Bronze Age	I	1900–1800 BC
	II	1800–1725 BC
	III	1725–1625 BC
Late Bronze Age	I	1625–1450 BC
	II	1450–1225 BC
	III	1225–1050 BC
Geometric	I	1050–950 BC
	II	950–850 BC
	III	850–750 BC
Archaic	I	750–600 BC
	II	600–475 BC
Classical	I	475–400 BC
	II	400–325 BC
Hellenistic		325–30 BC
Roman (Inauguration of Constantinople 330)		30 BC – AD 330
Late Roman (Second Arab raid 653/4)		AD 330–653/4
Political Status unclear (Intermittent Arab raids and Byzantine reoccupation)		AD 653/4–965
Byzantine (Usurpation of Isaac Comnenus 1184–91)		AD 965–1191
Richard Coeur-de-Lion } Knights Templars		AD 1191–1192
Lusignan		AD 1192–1489
Venetian		AD 1489–1571

Note The date and terminology for the Neolithic and Chalcolithic periods follow the scheme proposed by E. J. Peltenburg, *Levant* x (1978) 55ff. The Bronze Age dates are based on those suggested by R. S. Merimees, *RDAC* (1977) 33ff. In the Iron Age (Geometric to Classical) for the most part we have adopted Gjerstad's chronology outlined in *SCE* IV.2 except that we have raised the date of the beginning of the Archaic period to 750 BC which agrees with the findings of recent research.

Cypriote Art in the British Museum

Cyprus, set into the north-eastern corner of the Mediterranean Sea, is just within distant view of Syria to the east and Turkey to the north. The island is sufficiently far removed from the mainland to have allowed independent cultures to develop, although these were, at times, affected by influences from outside. Many of these influences were the result of trade, but sometimes they were initiated, or reinforced, by conquest or immigration. (See maps on page 32).

Stone Age/Neolithic and Chalcolithic Periods DAVID FRANKEL

The Earliest Settlements

So far as we know, the first people to settle on the island arrived in the seventh millennium BC. From their original homes in the northern Levant they brought a variety of domesticated plants (wheats, barley, legumes) and animals (pig, sheep, goat, fallow deer). At first they established themselves along the north and south coasts of the island, but later penetrated further into the well-forested interior.

This early colonisation seems to have been followed by a period of isolation, perhaps even of a decline in population, but during the fifth millennium BC other, new, settlers arrived, once again from the north-

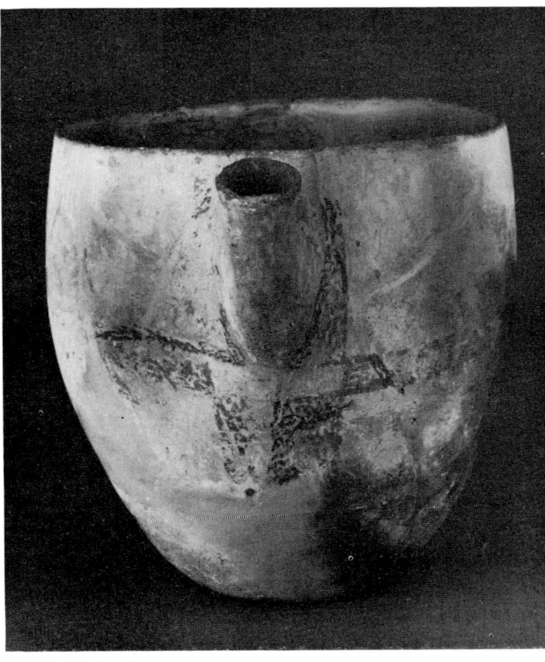

1 Chalcolithic spouted pot from Erimi. 1958.12–20.2. H.22.7cm.

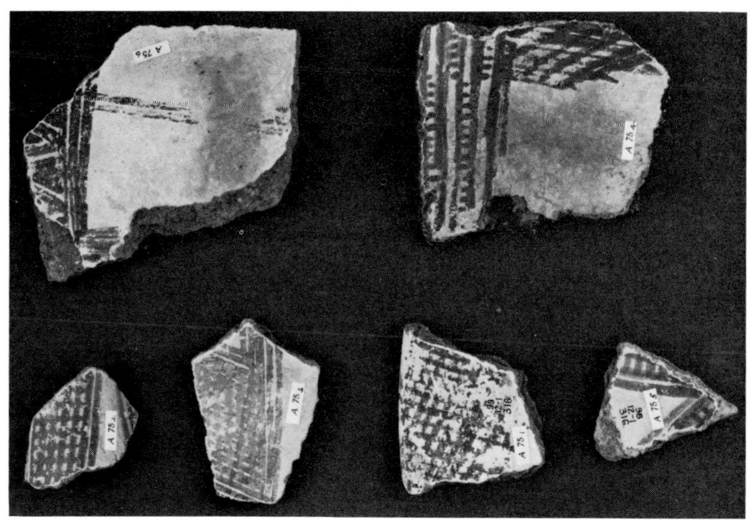

2 Group of Chalcolithic Red-on-White ware sherds from Kalavassos. 1898.12–1.313–318.

eastern coasts of the Mediterranean. Their initial coastal settlements were fortified, but the need for defence seems to have passed, and new settlements again spread inland to other, better-favoured areas.

The arts of these early, 'Neolithic' periods are, unfortunately, not represented in the British Museum. Although originally bringing pottery with them, the first settlers seem to have lost the techniques of making it and put much of their creative energy into working in stone, producing finely decorated bowls, and highly stylized human figures. With the advent of the new settlers, pottery was once again introduced to the island: from that time onward it remained a major medium for artistic expression.

After a period when only plain pottery was made, a variety of painted wares was developed in the late fifth millennium BC, which characterise cultural developments for about 1500 years. Within a basic tradition of decoration in red paint on a white ground many different styles and techniques were used: sometimes the red paint was combed when wet, to expose patterns in the white slip showing through from below; sometimes a multiple brush was used to produce a rippled pattern; sometimes fairly free brushwork is in evidence; but sometimes more formal decoration is seen. On the spouted pot (1) restrained horizontal and vertical bands cross one another, but most of the surface has been left plain. This careful style of painting is seen also on the sherds (2) which, like the pot, date from about 3000 BC, during the so-called 'Chalcolithic' phase, which is perhaps best known for the finely carved small stone figurines found at many sites *(see p. 5)*. The appearance of these figurines is one of several small changes which may be observed during the Chalcolithic Period in Cyprus. Another development was the introduction of copper tools, a few examples of which have been found in various excavations. This points towards contacts with other countries, although these cannot be precisely defined.

The Early and Middle Bronze Age

No sharp distinctions mark the transition from the last stages of the Chalcolithic to the succeeding 'Early Bronze Age' (or Early Cypriote Period'). In the accumulation of innovations noted from about 3000 BC it is possible to discern the roots of many features of the Early Cypriote Period. There are also some grounds for suggesting the importation of ideas (some archaeologists would even say a large-scale immigration) from Turkey, which prompted or accelerated the development of those features which are taken to mark the beginning of the 'Bronze Age'.

Adding to the problems of studying this transition is a difference in the nature of the available evidence, for, while the earlier periods are known primarily from excavations at settlements, the Early and Middle Bronze Age periods are known almost exclusively from cemeteries. This we owe, largely, to the nature of much early excavation, where information was of less concern than objects, and also to continuous looting of rich cemeteries and the need for rescue-excavations which this often imposes.

Cyprus during the Early Cypriote Period remained relatively isolated from surrounding areas. Later there were more contacts, particularly after about 1800 BC, but the small farming town or village continued to be the basis of Cypriote life and culture. Some fortified sites have been identified. These may well have served as refuges for villagers in the event of an attack from other areas of the island: the quantity of weapons found in tombs adds to the impression of at least occasional conflicts (3). The increase in the use of metal may also indicate that the rich copper sources for which the island is famous were beginning to be exploited, and is certainly one major economic development. Other changes, however, are less obvious. Pigs, for example, important in the agricultural economy of earlier periods declined in importance with the introduction of cattle (perhaps from Asia Minor). Cattle were not only better suited to the more open conditions resulting from several thousand years of human activity and forest clearance, but also provided a greater variety of produce as well as serving as a source of power. In

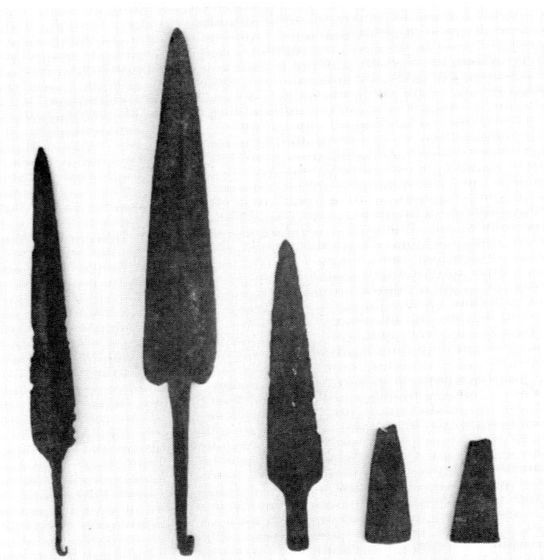

3 Selection of bronze weapons, knives and small axes. 1969.12–31.10, 14. L. 11.8, 29.5 cm; 1940.4–24.10, 3, 4. L.17.3, 6.7, 6.0 cm.

the Early Cypriote Period cattle became an important motif in art, and perhaps also in religion.

We know more, however, about burial practices than about other aspects of daily life. The dead were buried in underground chambers, hollowed out of soft limestone rock and reached by sloping entrance-passages. During the first phases of the Early Cypriote Period each tomb was used only once; later, larger tombs were made, which were used time and again over many years for successive burials. Many objects were placed with each burial: food, bronze tools and weapons, and, above all, pottery. Some of this pottery may have been made especially for the funeral, but much of it must have come from the household of the deceased, or from those of the mourners.

Although in some ways undesirable, the past concentration on cemetery evidence (itself a direct consequence of the attractive qualities of Cypriote art) has provided us with a wealth of material for archaeological and art-historical analysis. We may trace aspects of style and developments in techniques and note again a strong continuity in art and culture for over a thousand years from the start of the Early Cypriote Period in the mid-third millennium BC throughout the Middle Cypriote and into the Late Cypriote Period. Only the south-western areas of the island, where the pottery styles prevalent elsewhere were not adopted, stand outside the mainstream of this tradition, although some other regions (in particular the north-eastern Karpas Peninsula) were also clearly distinct. It is possible to look at the pottery of this period in many ways; here we may concentrate on isolating some general trends in the decoration on pots in order to define some of the aesthetic standards or rules which conditioned the artists' approach to their work when they produced objects acceptable to themselves and to the oothers of their villages.

The standard sequence of developments in pottery is based on the many finds from the large cemeteries on the north coast of the island. Potters of the Early Cypriote Period concentrated on producing red or red-and-black vessels with a smooth glossy surface obtained by burnishing the pots before firing. The earlier of these 'Red Polished' wares, following on the traditions of the Chalcolithic Period, tend to have flat bases and relatively tall, often fairly straight sides *(see p. 3)*; but gradually smaller bases, and later round bases and curved sides were favoured instead, so that by the end of the Early Cypriote Period the bodies of pots (particularly jugs and bowls) were approximately spherical. This slow change in what was considered aesthetically and functionally acceptable must have been effected by gradual and subtle changes in the manner of use of the vessels and in the techniques of manufacture.

Many of these Red Polished pots were decorated with geometric patterns incised in the surface with a sharp, pointed tool. On most these patterns were executed with great care and skill. Linear patterns, such as straight lines or zig-zags are usually found as parallel sets of lines. Some open designs, such as triangles or lozenges, are usually hatched, but sometimes there are concentric triangles and lozenges, just as there are concentric circles and semicircles. These design elements, used in a

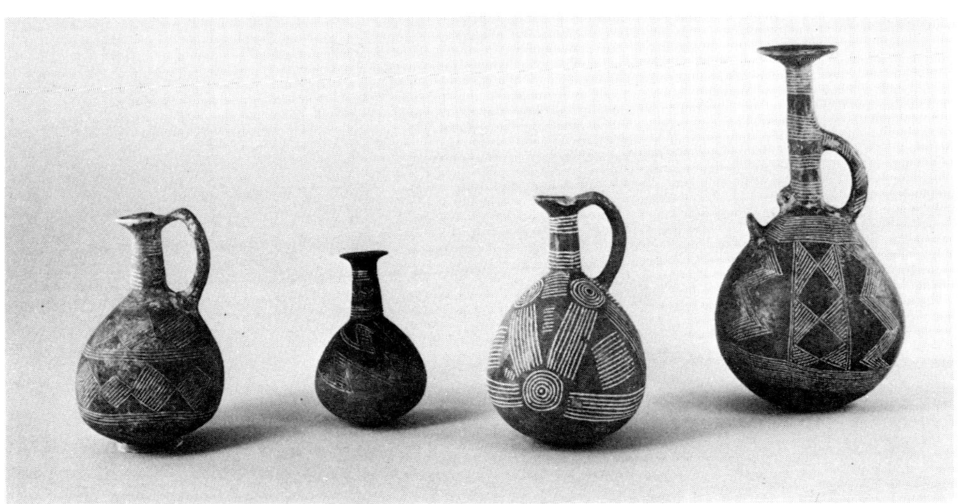

4 Red Polished ware vessels, with incised decoration. *BMC Vases* a) C66. H.14.6 cm; b) C75. H.11.4 cm; c) C65. H.15.8 cm; d) C64. H.24.8 cm.

variety of combinations, were built up into composite patterns, covering a large part of the surface of vessels; but this was not done at random, and it is possible to discern underlying structures and approaches to total design on many vessels.

To illustrate this we may look at a series of fine small round-based juglets with narrow necks, made during the high-point of Red Polished ware production, towards the end of the Early Cypriote Period and at the beginning of the Middle Cypriote Period. It is immediately clear that the pot is conceived of in three main sections – neck, body and base. The base is, as one might expect, the least important, and is normally left undecorated. Little attention is paid to the neck, which would normally have a simple series of sets of straight lines around it. The main decoration was reserved for the body, where the important zone of decoration was framed by sets of parallel lines. Within this space more complex decoration is found; we may define three main approaches by the potters to design in this section. One approach was to continue the system of divisions which separated the main zones by creating a series of horizontal bands within which rows of repeated design elements were placed, either in a more static (4a) or a more fluid (4b) arrangement. The second approach was to have a more flexible scheme, which is most often found when a fairly popular layout was employed (4c) with two rows of concentric circles diagonally and horizontally linked to one another. The third scheme was to provide a vertical aspect to the main zone. Here we find the greatest variety in motifs and variations in structure (4d).

The decoration on pots of other shapes was also conceived of in similar structured layouts, frequently repeating the scheme of a main, framed horizontal band of decoration, as on the shallow bowl *(see p. 2; left)*. On another bowl a somewhat different approach is evident *(see p. 2; right)*. These bowls, with their polished glossy surfaces, were generally fired red on the outside, and a rich deep black on the inside, which was otherwise left plain. Many have a small pierced lug at the rim, through which a string would have been threaded, so that the bowls could hang on the walls of houses when not in use.

Although Red Polished pottery was the most favoured during the Early Cypriote Period, other wares were also produced, including a painted style which picked up once more the old Chalcolithic tradition of Red-on-White decoration. The start of the 'Middle Cypriote Period' is marked by a resurgence in painted pottery, with the production of the first examples in a new tradition of 'White Painted' wares – painted in darker colour on a lighter ground. The earliest pots in this series have a polished, lustrous light orange slip, and the paint is fairly thick, often glossy, red. Later, however, as techniques and firing conditions changed a less glossy yellow or very light brown surface was more common, while the paint became a duller red-brown to grey. Eventually, by the beginning of the Late Cypriote Period, the surface of 'White Painted' pottery is off-white in colour and the paint a matt dark grey. Alongside these changes in surface treatment there are also small but cumulative changes both in shape and in decoration.

While the Early Cypriote White Painted wares display a thick, fairly free brushwork, contrasting with the patterns of incised decoration, the standard Middle Cypriote series of White Painted pottery is decorated in a more formal manner, as if the painters were using their brushes in the same way as the pointed tools used for incision. Their motifs retain the linear characteristics of incised techniques, and there was no real attempt to explore the possibilities of solid shape or form implicit in painting, but rather a reliance on motifs developed from within the repertoire found on incised vessels.

On the White Painted pots we may note again the tendency to divide vessels according to features of shape, to place less emphasis on the neck of jugs and to retain the main decoration for the body. The bases of the earliest White Painted vessels were normally covered all over with red colour, and so separated entirely from the rest of the body, but later this style was abandoned and the base, although still kept as a distinct field, was decorated. In contrast to the incised styles, there was a tendency to paint on all parts of the pots, including the bases, and the insides of shallow bowls.

As with Red Polished decoration, it is possible to distinguish several major regional styles in White Painted wares. A more free and open 'Wavy Line' style is the particular feature of the Karpas Peninsula (compare 7b). Simple vertical straight and wavy lines all around the bodies of pots are found most frequently in the eastern areas of the island (5a), where sets of angled lines crossing one another were also popular (5b). On the north coast, where the techniques were probably first developed, a heavier, more formal structure was retained (5c), while in the central areas of Cyprus several local styles share a number of features, including the use of many motifs, and a fairly formal structure in the layout of design (5d, e). In these more formal, or structured, styles the pots are often divided up to a greater extent than is the case with the incised traditions – employing not only the main horizontal units noted before, but also vertical divisions – breaking the vessel up into smaller fields of decoration, often halves, with a division in line with the handle, or quarters, with the addition of extra dividing lines at right-angles to the main handle-axis.

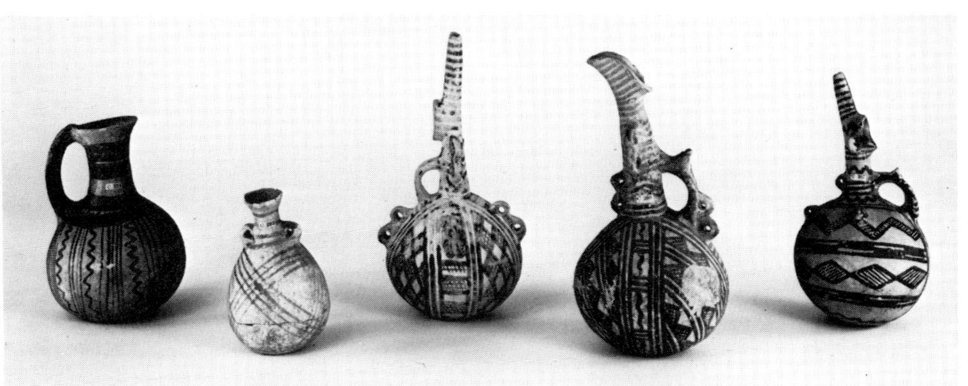

5 White Painted ware vessels. *BMC Vases* a) C274. H.12.0 cm; b) C292. H.9.5 cm; c) C288. H.18.0 cm; d) C280. H.18.3 cm; e) C287. H.16.4 cm.

In addition to the two main wares already discussed, many others were produced by the potters of the Middle Cypriote Period. Some were simply variants, such as the Black Polished vessels made during the latter stages of the Early and the first century of the Middle Cypriote Periods (6). These were much the same as the normal Red Polished pots, but were fired in a reducing atmosphere to give a deep, lustrous black surface instead of the standard red. Other wares were developed from the main traditions. During the course of the Middle Cypriote Period the fine quality Red Polished pots gradually gave way to Red Slip and Black Slip wares, with thinner, matt slips, and a new range of shapes. Although there was some better quality applied relief decoration, these wares tended to have simple, less carefully controlled incised patterns, often made with a small comb so that a number of parallel lines could be drawn at one time – allowing the artist to work more quickly and with less attention (7a).

6 Black Polished ware bottle. 1936.10–16.1. H.13.0 cm.

7 a) Late Red Polished ware amphora with incision using a comb. 1937.11–18.1. H.22.0 cm.
b) Red-on-Black ware jug, with painting using a multiple brush. 1937.3–17.1. H.5.0 cm.

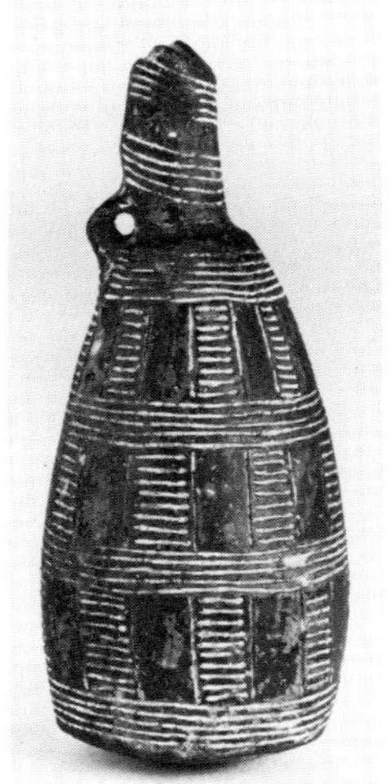

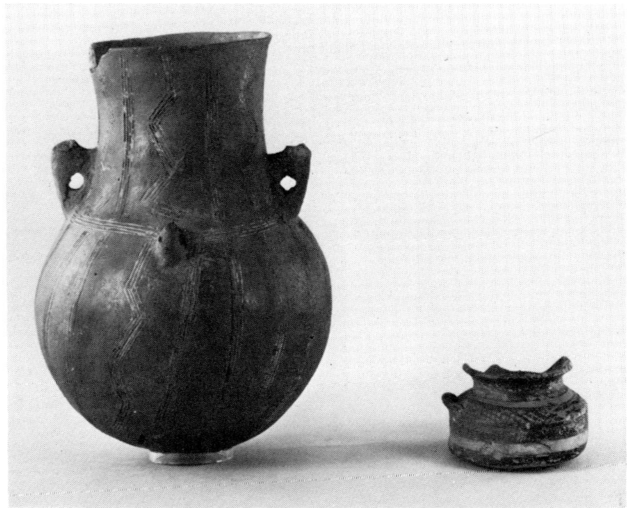

Similarly, there was a development in the use of multiple brushes – but this was a technique almost entirely restricted to the eastern region, particularly the Karpas Peninsula, where multiple brushes were often used to produce the simple sets of wavy, or wobbly lines characteristic of painting in that area. The Karpas was also the home of another fine painted ware – Red-on-Black (sometimes Red-on-Red) ware (7b). On many of these vessels the same style of decoration as on White Painted pottery is found, and multiple brushes with up to eighteen members were wielded by the artists with great care and to very great effect.

Within both the painted and incised traditions of pottery decoration there were some very common standard schemes of decoration that were used on a great many vessels. Nevertheless, despite the rules governing design structure and the varieties of motifs acceptable in each region, it was still possible for some artists to produce many varied compositions. Although hundreds – even thousands – of pots are known, it is only on rare occasions that two or more vessels are so alike, or betray so idiosyncratic a touch, that they can be confidently regarded as the work of the same person.

In all this wealth of decorated pottery there is only a handful of painted or incised human or animal representations, perhaps because of

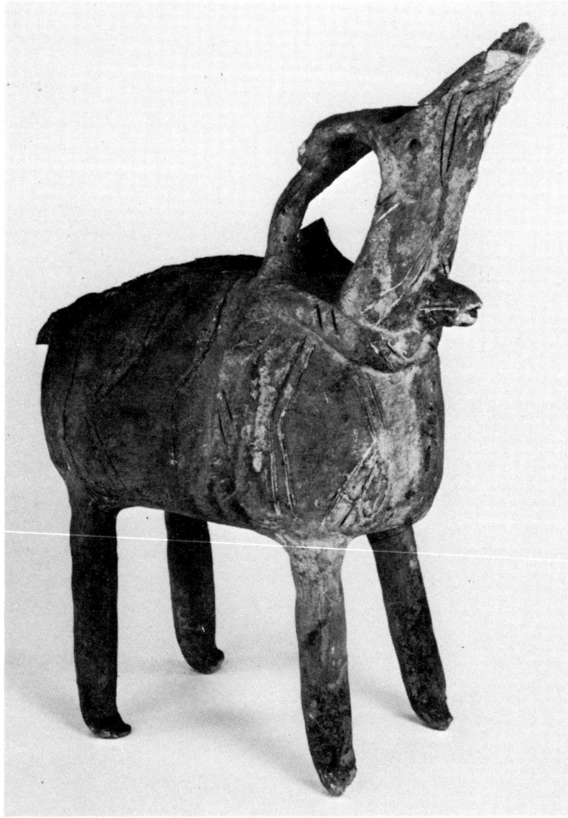

8 Large Red Polished ware pot in the shape of an animal 1925.11–1.2. H.30.2 cm.

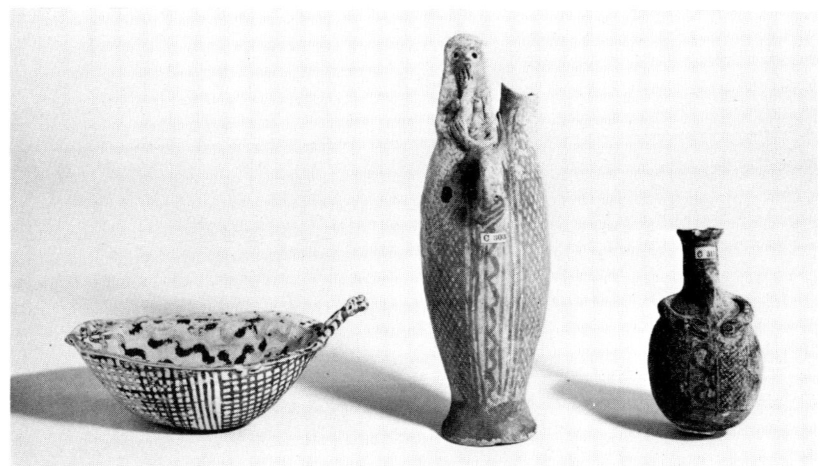

9 a) White Painted ware oval bowl with human figure on the rim. *BMC Vases* C 261. H. 5.0 cm.
b) White Painted ware bottle with top in the form of a human figure. *BMC Vases* C 303. H. 15.1 cm.
c) White Painted ware bottle in quasi-human form. *BMC Vases* C 311. H. 7.7 cm.

the difficulties in incising these forms, and the later reluctance to depart too far from the established geometric tradition. In complete contrast, when modelling in clay the potters felt both able and free to produce not only unusual and complex pots, but also to create a wide range of animal-shaped vessels (8) or to add animal forms to other pots, such as the earlier 'cult-vessel' *(see p. 3; right)*. Human figures were not negelected – they sometimes sit on the edge of bowls (9a), sometimes grow out of them (9b), and sometimes cannot decide whether they are pots, or people (9c).

There are also models of daily life, in which the people, and to a lesser extent the animals, are schematically rendered. The Red Polished figures in these models tend to be plain, while their White Painted counterparts are usually painted with horizontal stripes (perhaps purely decorative, but possibly reflecting personal body decoration of the period).

Besides these representations of people there is also a range of others with a different stylization: flat, generally rectangular, 'plank-idols'. Most of these, including ill. 10a with her cradled baby, are made in Red Polished ware, with incision used for some facial features, hair, ornaments, and clothing. There are fewer White Painted ware 'plank-idols' – a fragment (10b) is from an exceptionally large figure, which would have rivalled in size the few stone figures of similar shape. These, apart from a number of carvings (including one human figure) occasionally seen in the entrance shafts of tombs, are the only examples of Early or Middle Cypriote stone carvings so far found – a reminder that there must have been many art forms besides pottery of which we know nothing.

We still cannot be sure who made all the pottery we have been describing. Some archaeologists believe that there was a commercial production from the beginning of the Early Cypriote Period; but it is perhaps better to think in terms of a local household industry (perhaps

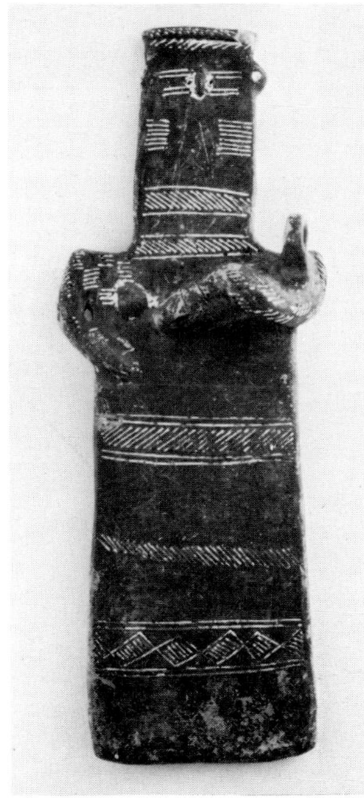 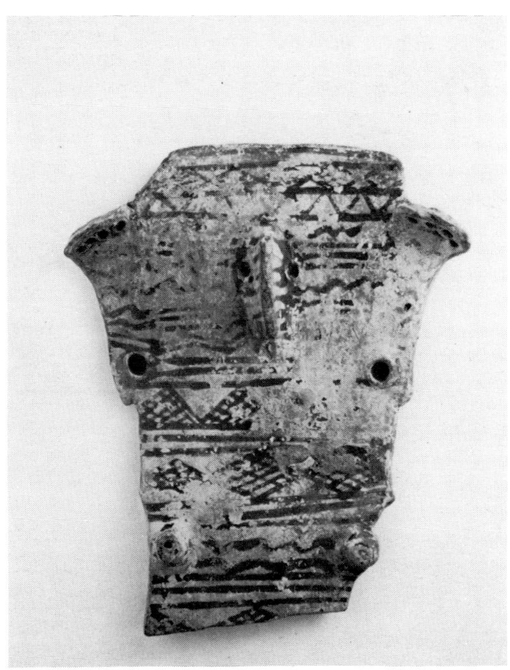

10 a) Red Polished ware plank idol. 1929.10–14.1. H.26.0 cm.
b) Fragment of White Painted ware plank idol. (New acquisition). H.17.0 cm.

with women potters) at least until well into the Middle Cypriote Period, when the increase in the simpler styles characteristic of the east of the island may indicate a growth in mass production. White Painted pottery from this part of Cyprus was traded across the sea to the Levantine mainland, where it has been found at many sites, demonstrating also increasingly important trade contacts in the later stages of the Middle Cypriote Period. These external contacts are part of a gradual change in the economic and cultural orientation of the island, which was becoming less isolated and more a part of the wider Eastern Mediterranean world. Unlike the earlier artistic traditions, the arts of the succeeding Late Cypriote Period cannot be looked at in so self-contained a manner, for the earlier tribal art was giving way to more commercial production affected by the growth of larger towns, and by the influences from abroad.

Late Bronze Age

The Late Cypriote Period, as defined by archaeologists, begins towards the end of the seventeenth century BC. No sudden change marks this new 'period' but there was, rather, a gradual evolution in pottery styles and metalwork leading to the establishment of distinctive new types. Although slow it was not necessarily a peaceful development, as the less formal relationships between smaller settlements gave way to larger political units and a more organised exploitation and distribution of

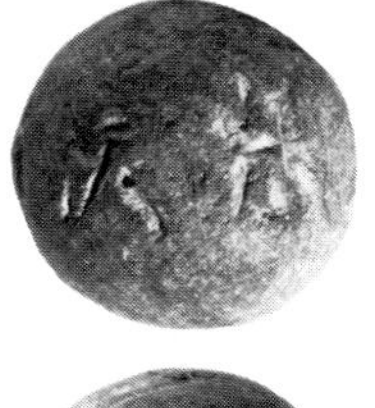
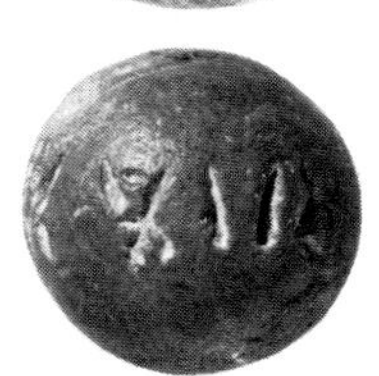
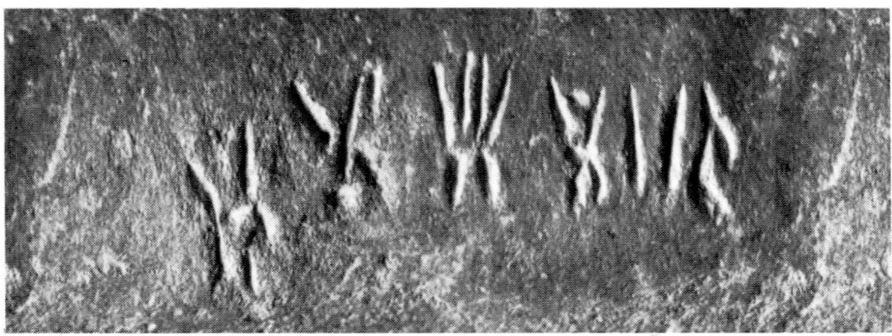

11 a) Cypro-Minoan script on a clay ball from Hala Sultan Tekke. 1898.12–1.204.
b) Periphery photograph of script.

copper. Some areas, such as the north coast, became less important, while elsewhere cities grew up, particularly along the eastern and southern coasts of the island. This spread of settlement may be linked to an ecological change brought about by a lowering of the sea-level and the consequent drying-out of previously swampy low-lying areas; the development of larger urban centres reflects the increase in overseas trade, channelled through these ports.

It is generally assumed that copper was the major Cypriote export, but many other goods were also involved in the complex patterns of trade and diplomacy in the Eastern Mediterranean. Strong links were maintained with the city-states of the Levant, and from the fifteenth century BC there were also important trade contacts with the Mycenaean world of Greece. A more sophisticated urban society and the influx of goods, ideas and technology from abroad created within Cyprus a demand for a wider range of products and an appreciation of varied art-styles. A local script developed, as written records became essential for commerce and administration, but as this has not yet been fully deciphered we are still not even sure what language was spoken by the Cypriots of this period (11).

For the first few hundred years of the Late Cypriote Period the people of Cyprus were essentially the descendants of the earlier Bronze Age inhabitants but in the last 150 years this was changed. From about 1200 BC major social disruptions in Greece led many people to seek new homes elsewhere, including Cyprus. These population movements, linked to those of the various groups known collectively as the 'Sea Peoples', affected all areas in the Eastern Mediterranean; Cyprus did not escape its share of violence, and it is probable that the older population suffered greatly at the hands of the new settlers from Greece.

Cities such as Enkomi and Kition best reveal the cosmopolitan and sophisticated urban life of this period of Mycenaean or Achaean Greek settlement in the twelfth and eleventh centuries BC, with their large-scale architecture and wealth of luxury goods, both locally produced and imported from many other lands. The older local styles and traditions were more or less submerged. Similarly with the arrival of successive groups of Greek-speaking immigrants, Greek must have replaced the earlier Cypriote language.

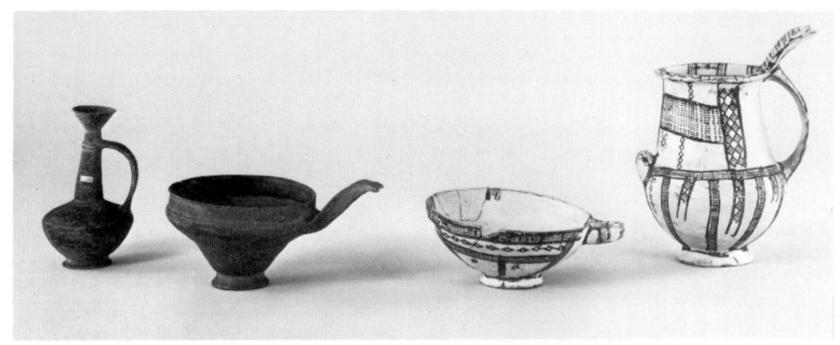

12 a) Base-Ring ware juglet. *BMC Vases* C113. H.14.0 cm. b) Base-Ring ware bowl. *BMC Vases* C121. H.8.4 cm. c) White Slip ware bowl. *BMC Vases* C233. H.6.7 cm, D.14.2 cm. d) White Slip ware tankard. *BMC Vases* C245. H.21.0 cm.

Turning now to the arts of the period, we may begin with pottery. There were two main fine wares characteristic of the Late Cypriote Period – 'Base Ring' ware (12a, b), and 'White Slip' ware (12c, d). These were technically superior to earlier pottery, and were probably mass-produced. Although the potter's-wheel was known and used in Cyprus, these vessels, like earlier ones, were formed using hand-building techniques.

Small 'Base-Ring' ware juglets similar to ill. 12a were exported to Egypt and the Levant, as containers for oil, perfumes, or, more probably, opium as the shape of the vessel may be thought of as representing a poppy-head, advertising the contents. Other pots, however, were not exported as containers, but as objects in their own right. White Slip bowls (12c) were popular items in the cities of the Levant, where their assymetrical shape and neat but slightly imperfect decoration set them off from the plainer local wares, and from the other major type of imported pottery – Mycenaean wares. From the fifteenth century onward, Mycenaean pottery of extremely high quality was traded from Greece all over the Eastern Mediterranean, and was imported in large quantities into Cyprus. There it was imitated by some potters, some of whose products are so close to the imported pots in both quality and technique that they are almost indistinguishable.

In general, pots produced in older Cypriote traditions continued to be painted with geometric motifs, while those of imported types often have representational scenes. Bulls and chariots are frequently to be found on Mycenaean vessels (13a, b), which may have been produced in Greece especially for the eastern market. The greater use of two-dimensional representations is seen on other objects as well – for example faience vessels, some of which were made on the island, after the manner of those imported from Egypt *(see title page)* or other areas of the Near East.

With three-dimensional figures, we do not find in the later period any of the earlier 'plank-idols' although some other local forms continue. There is, rather, a local adaptation of a Syrian type of female figure (14) of quite another style. Whether this change in form reflects a change in the attitude to, or the use of, the figure is unclear. Besides terracotta figures there are also some extremely fine statuettes made in copper or bronze. These, like the fine decorated bronze stand (15) (one of a series

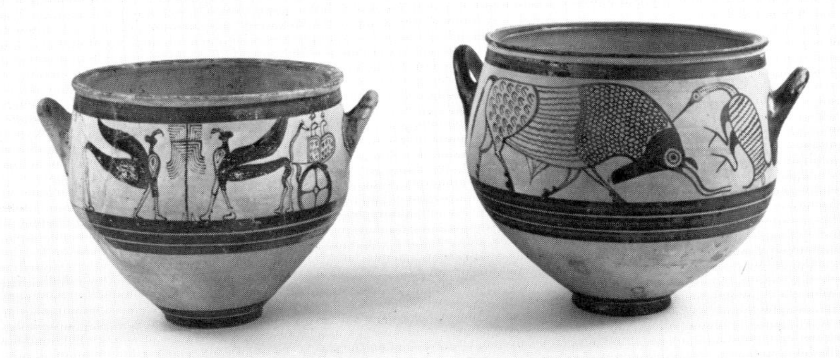

13 Mycenaean ware craters. a) from Enkomi Tomb 48. *BMC Vases* C 397. H.24.3 cm. b) from Enkomi Tomb 83. *BMC Vases* C 416. H.26.2 cm.

which may all be the work of a particularly skilful craftsman) all testify to new technical abilities. These contrast with the metal products of the earlier periods, which, although exceptionally numerous, are almost entirely utilitarian, and produced by the simplest of techniques. This expansion of the metal industry is matched by that of other crafts; the variety of techniques and objects makes it difficult to do more than mention the more important of them.

One of the crafts to develop in Cyprus during this period was seal-cutting. The growth of commerce and organised administration in the Late Cypriote Period led to a need for seals to authenticate documents or establish ownership. Drawing on both older Near Eastern and the later

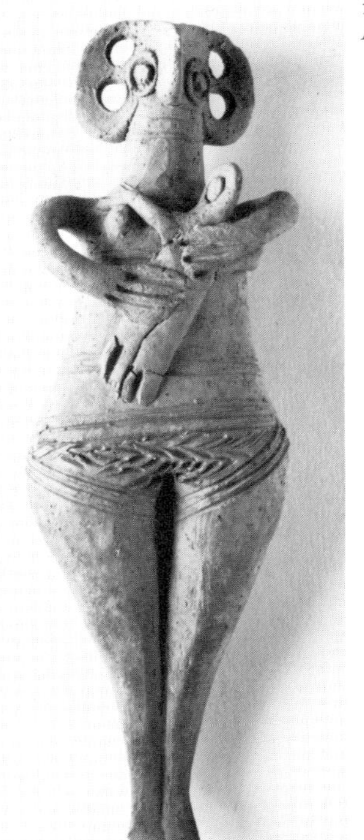

14 Terracotta figurine from Enkomi. *BMC Terracottas* A 11. H.19.5 cm.

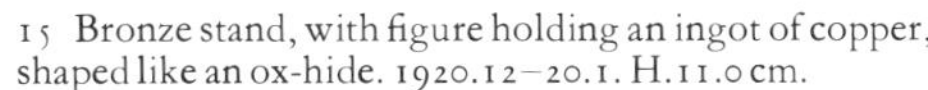

15 Bronze stand, with figure holding an ingot of copper, shaped like an ox-hide. 1920.12–20.1. H.11.0 cm.

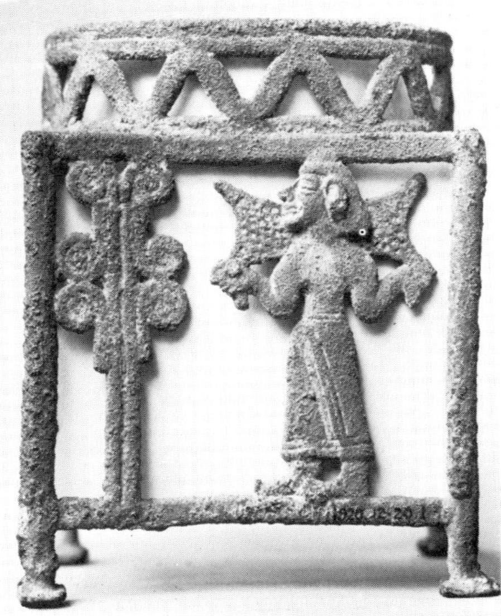

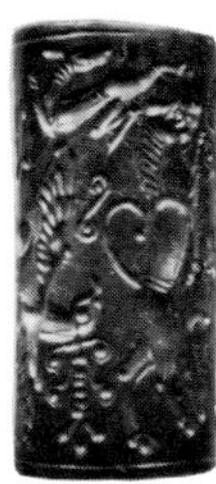
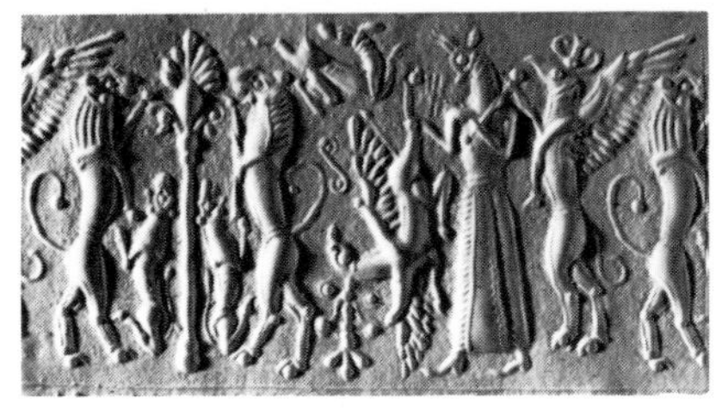

16 Late Cypriote cylinder seal and impression made from it, from Hala Sultan Tekke. 1898.12–1.198. L.2.9 cm.

Mycenaean traditions, a local style of cylinder seal developed in Cyprus. The seal (16) illustrated here is a particularly fine example in the main line of Cypriote development, combining a variety of elements, some derived from the east, others from the west.

Ivory was often used for luxury goods in many parts of the ancient world. Cyprus was no exception, and some extremely fine examples, demonstrating either Aegean or eastern styles of decoration have been found. The ivory gaming-box (17) made for an originally Egyptian game, was decorated on the sides with scenes of vigorous action. The galloping animals have been compared with those of the Aegean area, but the details of the chariots and the people in them are clearly of the east.

Jewellery too, was produced in larger quantities especially toward the last stages of the Late Cypriote Period. Rings, ear-rings (18a), and necklaces (18b) are among the many forms of jewellery known. Many of these again show cosmopolitan styles, although most can be traced to eastern rather than to western, Mycenaean, origins. Decorated gold diadems and pectorals (18c), for example, developed from Near Eastern forms, although the designs stamped on them may, like the sphinxes with their plumed crowns (compare 13a), derive from the Mycenaean world, as much as from other areas. Among the more typically Mycenaean objects is the pomegranate-shaped pendant (18d), while the finger-ring (18e) is obviously Egyptian. The pin (18f) with its gold-wire shaft giving a plaited effect seems to be a particular local Cypriote form, although the general type is eastern.

17 Ivory gaming-box from Enkomi. 1897.4–1.996. L.29.1 cm.

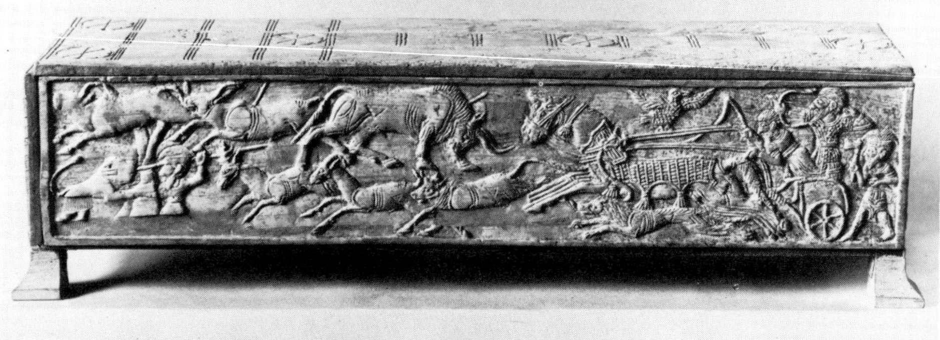

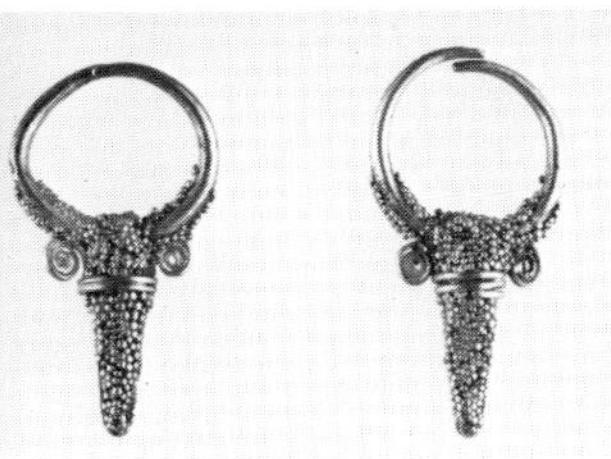

18 a) Ear-rings from Maroni. *BMC Jewellery* 538. L.2.8 cm.
b) Necklace from Enkomi. *BMC Jewellery* 580. L.35.0 cm.
c) Gold pectoral embossed with sphinxes, from Enkomi. *BMC Jewellery* 196. L.9.1 cm, W.5.0 cm.
d) Gold pendant from Enkomi. *BMC Jewellery* 623. L.3.6cm.
e) Ring with the name of the Egyptian goddess Mut. *BMC Finger-rings* 1. D.2.2 cm.
f) Dress-pin of twisted gold wire. *Marshall Jewellery* 550. L.13.2 cm.

All these fine luxury goods demonstrate clearly the wealth and the overseas trading connections of Cyprus, particularly during the last 150 years of the Late Cypriote Period. Although prosperous, this was not a peaceful time. Conditions in the Eastern Mediterranean were generally unsettled, and the cities of Cyprus were among those that suffered destructions. These may have been caused by raids of various groups of 'Sea Peoples' or may demonstrate some attempts by the indigenous population to reassert themselves. Finally, at the end of the Late Cypriote Period, about 1050 BC, many older cities were abandoned. Memories of the Mycenaean Greek colonisation were, however, preserved in a series of foundation legends by the people of later times, and a degree of continuity can be traced in many other respects as well.

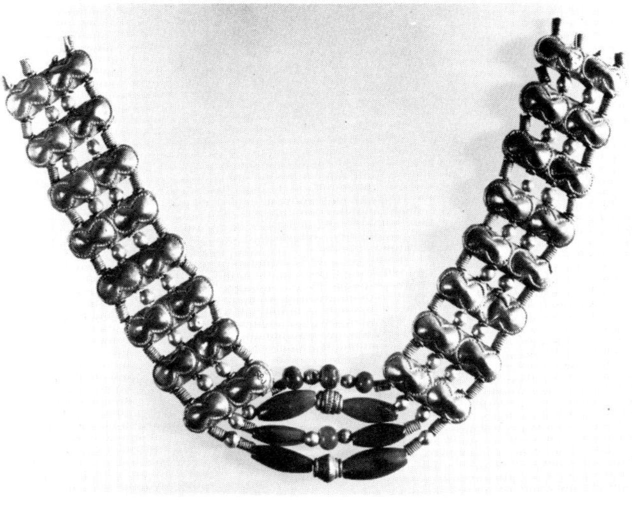

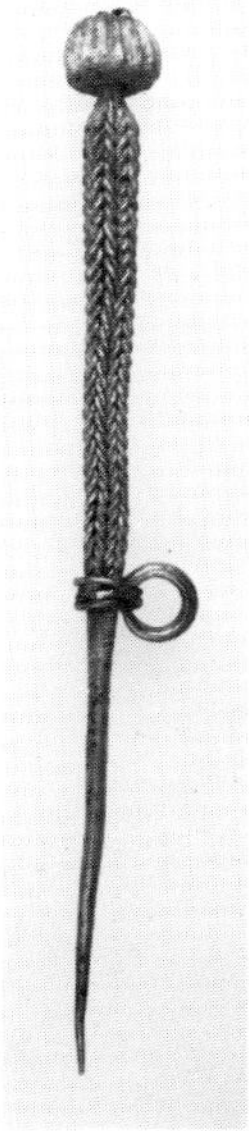

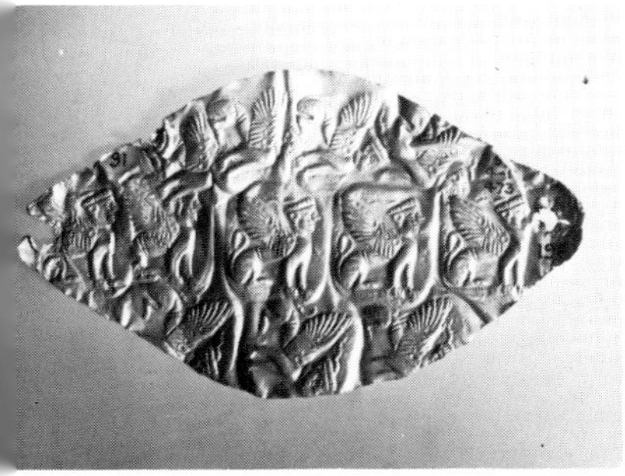

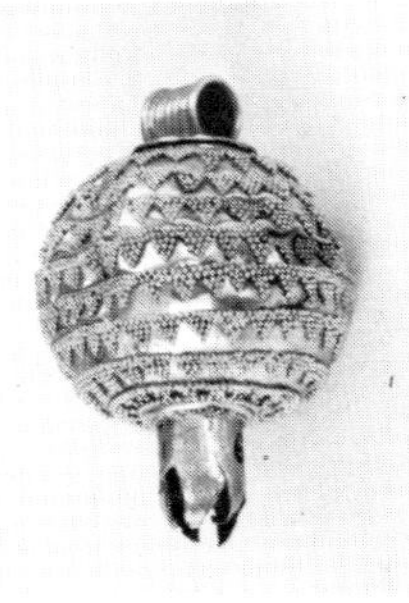

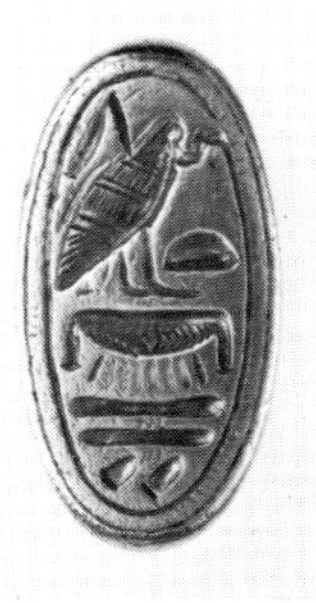

The Geometric Period

The transition from the Bronze to the Iron Age in Cyprus is normally placed in the mid-eleventh century BC. It is marked by no event of great moment but rather by a general decline in prosperity and the virtual abandonment of several major sites. The first part of the eleventh century had seen the island as a prosperous centre with commercial connections with the Near East and the Aegean. Refugees including Cretans arrived from the Mycenaean world to settle in Cyprus, bringing with them new pottery styles and tomb types. In return Cyprus may have played some part in introducing iron-working to the Aegean in the earlier eleventh century since, when the Iron Age begins in Cyprus, the metal itself had already been in use for about a century.

Therefore the dawn of the Iron Age finds a mixed population in the island with new arrivals living alongside those Cypriots who had survived the calamities. The Early Iron Age settlements are often close to their Late Bronze Age predecessors and occasionally there is evidence for continuous occupation as at Palaepaphos and Kourion. Squatters continued to live at Enkomi although the main population moved closer to the sea to Salamis which was founded in the earlier eleventh century BC. At Kition the Iron Age settlement was to occupy the same site as its Bronze Age predecessor, but after the end of the eleventh century it was evidently deserted for 150 years. New settlements were established at Lapithos and Marion in the north and, in the tenth century BC, at Amathus in the south. The latter was probably founded by native Cypriote refugees (known as the Eteo-Cypriots) from abandoned Late Bronze Age centres.

For the first 200 years (Cypro-Geometric I and II) Cyprus was in a 'dark age'. The information available generally comes from cemeteries

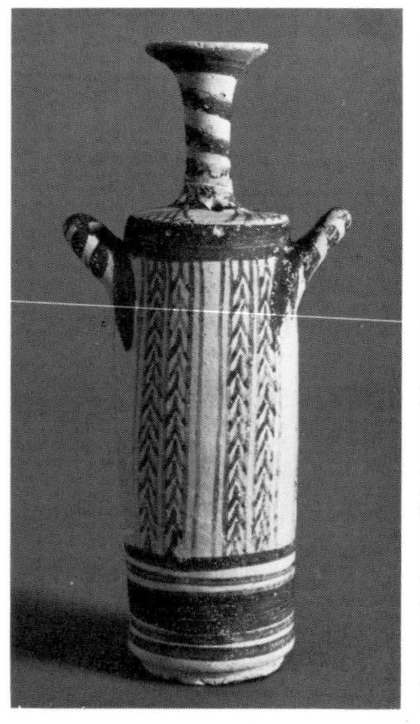

19 Two-handled bottle, White Painted ware. 1000–900 BC. 1929.10–14.3. H.23.0 cm.

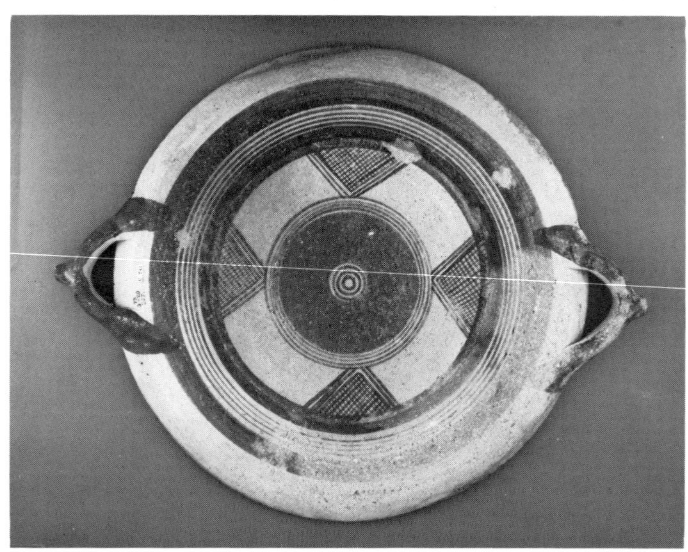

20 Plate, Bichrome ware, from Idalion. 900–800 BC. *BMC Vases* C741. D.27.1 cm.

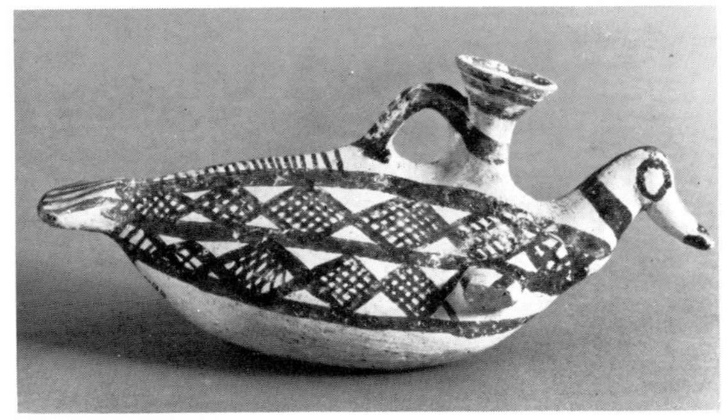

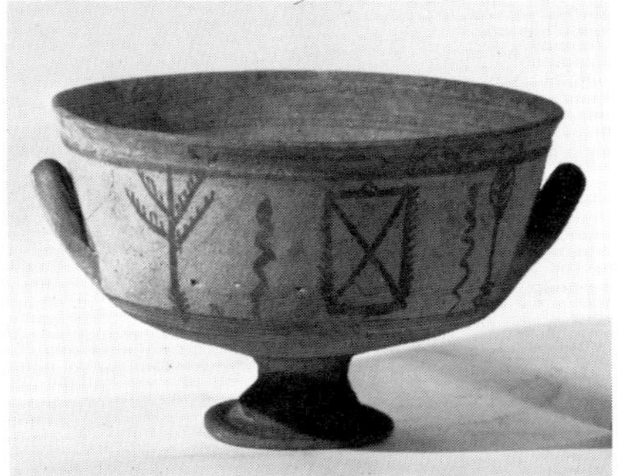

21. Bird-shaped bottle, White Painted ware. 1100–1000 BC. 1927.12–13.2. L.22.0 cm.

22 Stemmed bowl, Bichrome ware. 850–750 BC. 1936.12–30.1. H.10.25 cm.

rather than settlements, and we therefore know little about domestic life. Burials were still inhumations in rock-cut chamber tombs, which were often used for more than one generation of a family. However, notably at Kourion and Lapithos, tombs of Mycenaean-type with long narrow entrance passages (*dromoi*) are found alongside Cypriote chamber tombs in the Bronze Age tradition.

The Aegean refugees who arrived about 1100 BC introduced the Proto-White Painted pottery of the end of the Late Cypriote Bronze Age whose shapes and ornaments are for the most part of Late Mycenaean and Minoan (Cretan) origin. Influence from the Levant accounts for certain types but more particularly for the Bichrome technique, which appeared in the island about the same time. The fine pottery of the initial stages of the Iron Age (Cypro-Geometric I–II), has its origins in these Late Bronze Age fabrics. Most common are White Painted ware with the ornaments shown in matt black or brown on a buff or greenish-white slip (19, 21, 23, 24) and Bichrome ware which adds decoration in matt red (20, 22). The decoration is principally geometric, usually arranged in

23 Amphora neck, White Painted ware, from Kition. 800–750 BC. *BMC Vases* C858, C859. H.15.2 cm (both).

24 Barrel jug, White Painted ware. 1000–900 BC. 1876.9–9.74. H.36.8 cm.

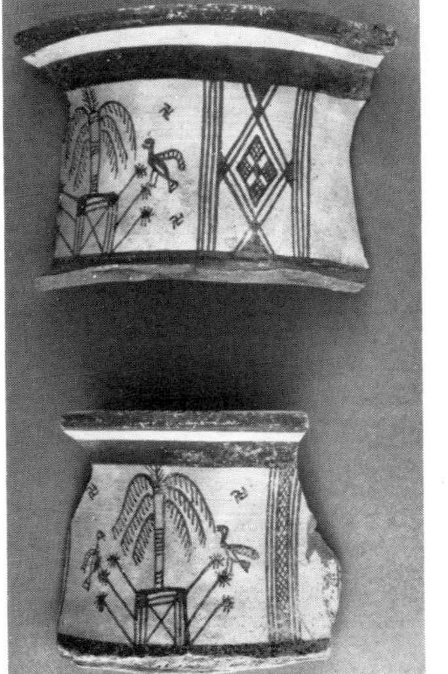

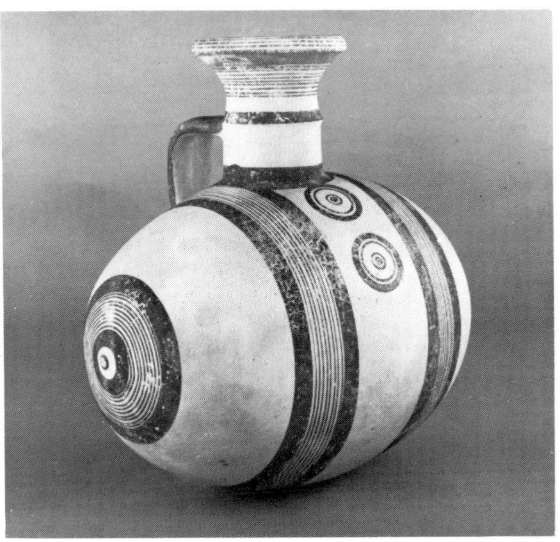

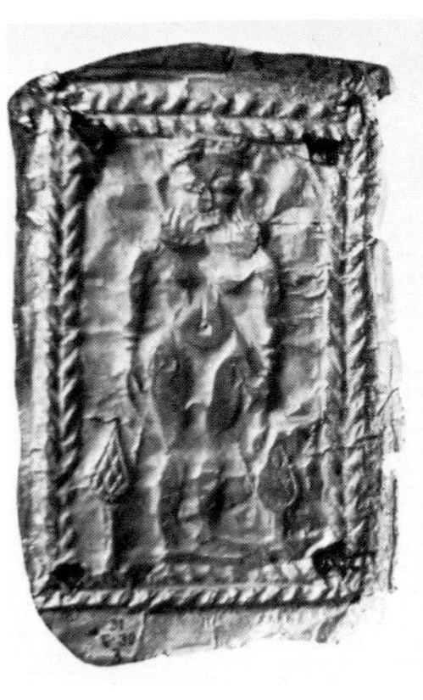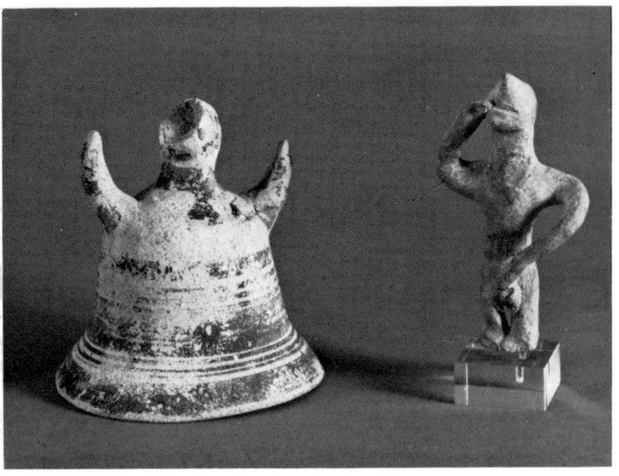

25 Gold plaque with repoussé decoration. 800–750 BC. *BMC Jewellery* 1487. L.5.3, W.3.4 cm.

26 a) Terracotta figurine from Kourion. 900–800 BC. *BMC Terracottas* A 5. H.8.2 cm.
b) Terracotta figurine from Amathus. 800–750 BC. *BMC Terracottas* A 214. H.8.2 cm.

bands, zones or panels, although sometimes the body of the vessel is left plain apart from encircling bands. The shapes like the fabrics often follow those found in the Proto-phases and include two-handled bottles (19), low dishes with wishbone handles showing the principal decoration on the underside (20) and bird-shaped flasks (21). Other popular forms are stemmed bowls (22) and large amphorae decorated in panels on the neck (23). The ornaments include schematic animals, which have their origin in Late Minoan Crete, but our illustration (23) showing birds either side of a 'tree of life' is of Near Eastern inspiration. New are the barrel-shaped jugs with ridges on the handle decorated with concentric circles (24). These are evidently developed from Syro-Palestinian lentoid bottles of the end of the Bronze Age, which had themselves been imitated in Cypriote Proto-White Painted and Proto-Bichrome ware.

The poverty of the period is reflected in the comparatively poor grave goods. However, some gold-work survives including embossed plaques with folded edges. These evidently formed part of a *polos*, a Syrian headdress, and the decoration is likewise often of Near Eastern inspiration, showing 'Astarte'-type figures (Astarte was the Eastern mother goddess) (25). The terracottas are simple 'snowman figures', small and handmade with peg-like heads and schematic bodies (26a). Towards the end of the geometric period a new type with wheel-made bell-shaped bodies and peg-like heads appears (26b).

Commercial ties with the Near East had been maintained through the 'dark age' and we have observed Eastern influence on Cypriote pottery and jewellery. In the ninth century the Phoenicians came to settle, at least at Kition, and contacts with the Aegean were renewed. Consequently there was a general revival and re-emergence of Cypriote culture. The date and extent of the Phoenician colonisation of Cyprus and the West is still debated. However, recent excavations at Kition have revealed two large Phoenician temples built in the second half of the ninth century and we know from documentary evidence that that city was under Syrian rule by the end of the eighth century BC. The typical Phoenician Black-on-Red pottery, the ornaments painted in black on a red ground, now

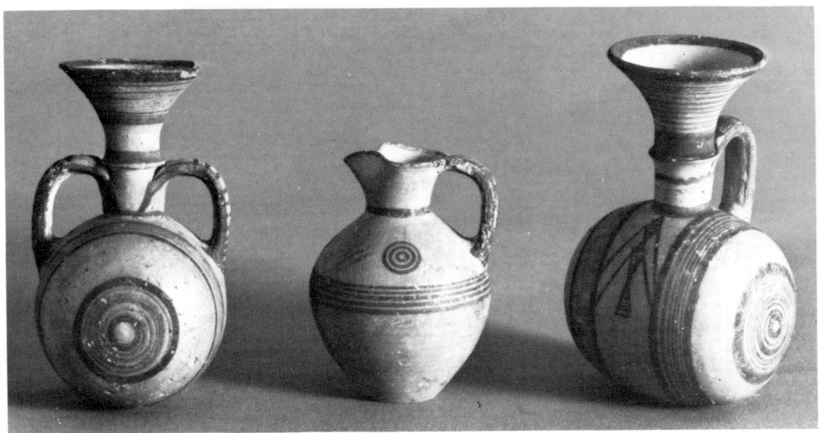

27 Black-on-Red ware. 800–750 BC.
a) Two-handled barrel flask from Amathus. *BMC Vases* C 895. H.9.6 cm.
b) Jug from Amathus. *BMC Vases* C 885. H.7.4 cm.
c) Jug, no provenance. 1908.4–11.39. H.10.0 cm.

began to be made locally by the Cypriots. The early shapes often imitate those in the corresponding Bichrome and White Painted fabrics; we find jugs with handle-ridges decorated with concentric circles and sometimes with linear ornaments opposite the handle (27c) and two-handled globular flasks (27a). New shapes include footless deep bowls with simple linear decoration and flat-bottomed jugs with horizontal bands around the belly and groups of concentric circles above (27b). Both of these last are typically Phoenician shapes, which in turn were imitated by the Cypriots in their White Painted and Bichrome fabrics. In general the vases are of a higher quality, the shapes more articulate and the ornaments more carefully and concisely drawn. In addition first attempts are made at a pictorial style. In the eighth century the Cypriots became literate again and the first inscriptions in the Cypriote syllabic script are recorded. It had between fifty and sixty characters and was used to write both Greek and Eteo-Cypriote (the native tongue surviving from the Bronze Age). It was evidently related in some way to the Cypro-Minoan script of the Late Bronze Age.

The general revival of Cypriote culture is accompanied by an increase in population. Kition, as we have seen, was re-occupied after a gap of 150 years. At Salamis the first of the monumental 'royal' tombs was under construction in the second quarter of the eighth century, again evidence of activity after over a century of obscurity. Sites like Golgoi and Tamassos were re-occupied for the first time since the Bronze Age, and the population of others like Ayia Irini and Idalion grew at the end of Cypro-Geometric III, looking forward to their zenith in the Archaic Period.

The Archaic Period

The Archaic Period is the most glorious in the history of Cypriote art in the Iron Age. The island was subjected to a number of foreign powers, which in turn enriched the Cypriote repertoire, while the Cypriots themselves played an increasingly important role in international affairs, acting as an intermediary between east and west. In the mid-eighth century Assyria emerged as the major power and under Tiglath-Pileser III showed increasing aggression towards its neighbours, extending its sphere of influence in Syria, Phoenicia and Palestine. Finally in 709 BC Sargon II, the successor of Tiglath-Pileser III, brought Cyprus to submission. An inscribed stele (relief slab of stone) from Kition, now in Berlin, names seven city kingdoms in Cyprus that paid homage. In later Assyrian records we read of ten kingdoms. These city kingdoms grew and flourished independently of each other and were later to strike their own coinages and be divided in their loyalties. Assyrian domination lasted some fifty years until about 669 BC when the Assyrian Empire began to break up. There followed nearly a century of independence during which Cypriote art and culture developed in its own right. In about 569 BC Amasis, the Egyptian Pharaoh, took political control of the island. This, however, was to last less than thirty years, as in 545 BC Cyprus voluntarily submitted to Persia, whose empire now stretched westwards to include the East Greek cities of Ionia. Although Cyprus became part of the fifth satrapy of the Persian Empire in 521 BC, the island at first retained a considerable degree of independence. However, in 498 BC it took part in the Ionian revolt, an attempt by the East Greek cities to break away from Persian rule. Cyprus suffered badly and several cities were besieged. Pro-Persian kings were placed on the thrones of the city kingdoms and the Cypriots were forced to support the Persian forces in their operations against Greece.

The domination of Cyprus by three foreign powers in comparatively quick succession left its mark on Cypriote culture. The island also played an increasing part in international trade and Cypriote goods were exported notably to the islands of Rhodes and Samos. Before the period of Egyptian rule (569–545 BC) Cyprus came into contact with the Egyptian world through its close relations with Naucratis, a Greek trading post established in the Egyptian delta. A number of products from the Levant imported or imitated by the Cypriots reached not only the Greek world but also Phoenician centres in the Western Mediterranean. It is not always easy to determine the exact role of Cyprus in this international market, but it certainly acted as an intermediary to some extent. That Cyprus itself was prosperous is amply borne out by the 'royal' tombs at Salamis. These had stone-built chambers and facades, and were furnished with rich grave goods. Horses were sometimes slaughtered and buried with chariots or hearses in the *dromoi* (entrance passages), recalling burial customs described by Homer. Similar tombs were built elsewhere in the island at this time while Phoenician Kition continued to flourish.

Cypriote art naturally reflects the trends that have been outlined. Decorated metal bowls are among the finest products. The example illustrated here (28) was found at Amathus and dates from the seventh

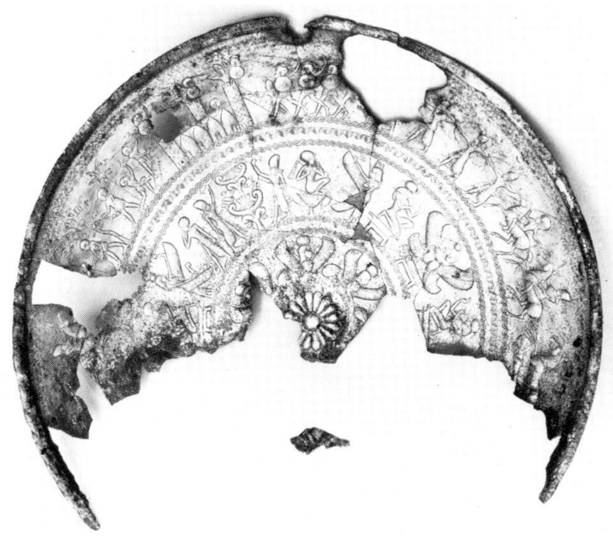

28 Silver bowl from Amathus. 700–600 BC. WAA 123053. D.20.5 cm.

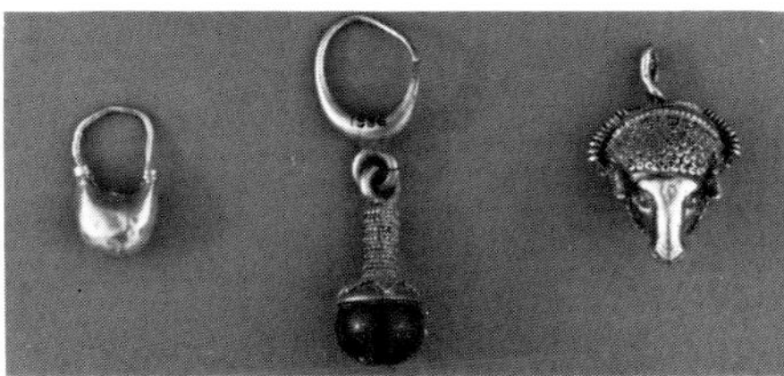

29 a) Gold ear-ring, from Marion. 700–600 BC. *BMC Jewellery* 1593. L.1.8 cm.
b) Gold ear-ring, from Amathus. 600–500 BC. *BMC Jewellery* 1596. L.4.1 cm.
c) Gold pendant seal, from Marion. 550–500 BC. *BMC Jewellery* 1599. D. (disk) 1.4 cm.

century. The outer frieze may illustrate a forgotten scene from Phoenician or Syrian mythology and, as we shall see, vase painters adopted similar motifs borrowed from Syria and Phoenicia. Cypriote craftsmen would certainly have been capable of producing a work of this high quality at this time, and the present writer believes that this and other decorated metal bowls from the island are of local manufacture.

Jewellers for the most part continued the types which were by now well established in the Cypriote repertoire. Ear-rings with tapered hoops had already been made in the Late Bronze Age and the finds from Geometric contexts, although not numerous, show that the form survived through the 'dark age'. The Archaic examples are more elaborate. Some have pendants decorated with rich granulation (grains of metal soldered on to a background) which was a popular decorative technique for fine jewellery in this period (29b). The boat-shaped type (29a) with a hollowed hoop to which the pin was attached has been found in seventh-century contexts in East Greece including Ephesus, where it was apparently adopted from Syria. It is not certain whether the Cypriote examples were made locally or imported from East Greece, but it is clear that they were familiar in Cyprus since they are worn by Cypriote sculptures both as ear-rings and occasionally as nose-rings. The pendant seal from Marion (29c) is a 'pseudo-scarab' probably imported from East Greece in the second half of the sixth century.

The vases are perhaps the best guide to the regional differences in Archaic Cyprus. The attractive pictorial style (30–2), which had begun at the end of the Geometric Period, was now characteristic of the

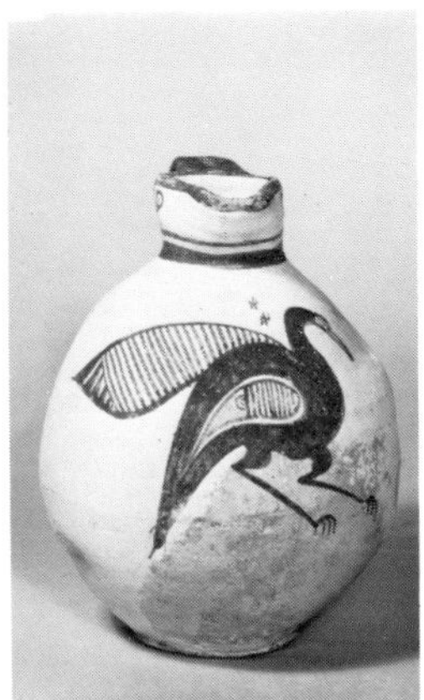

30 Jug, Bichrome ware;
decorated in the 'free field' style,
about 700 BC. 1929.2–11.2.
H.18.0 cm.

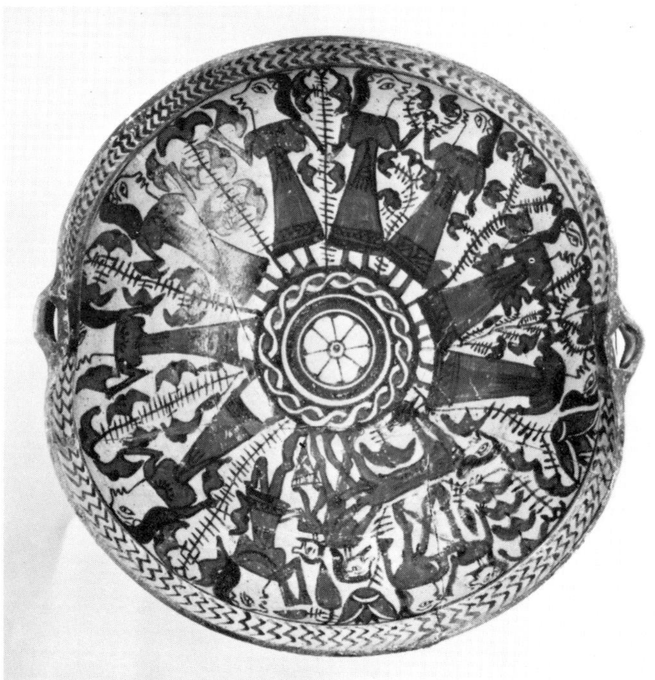

31 Bowl, Bichrome ware, from Achna, about 600 BC. *BMC Vases* C838.
H.10.9 cm, D.34.3 cm.

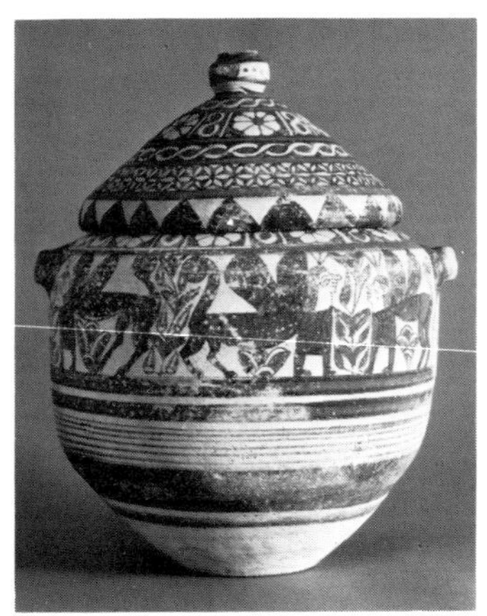

32 Pyxis (box), Bichrome ware, from
Achna, about 600 BC. *BMC Vases*
C839. H.24.8 cm, D. (with cover) 33.9
cm.

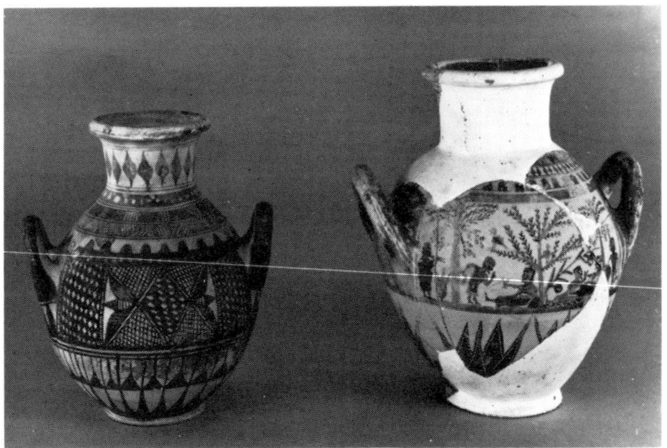

33 a) Amphora, Bichrome ware, from Amathus. 550–500 BC. *BMC
Vases* C851. H.19.7 cm.
b) Amphora, White Painted ware, from Amathus. 550–500 BC. *BMC
Vases* C855. H.22.7 cm.

southern and eastern areas of the island. The shapes are mostly developed from their precursors and the favourite fabrics are still White Painted and Bichrome. The scenes show a wide variety of compositions drawing their inspiration from Syrian and Phoenician textiles and metalwork. Jugs may be decorated in the 'free-field' style with no ground line, and birds are a favourite motif (30). The vases from Amathus form a particular group. Belly-handled amphorae decorated with elaborate ornaments packed closely together are popular (33a). A variation is illustrated by the 'picnic vase' (33b), which shows an attempt by the artist to portray a symposium in the Greek manner. There are a few other examples from different sites showing deliberate imitations of Greek motifs. In the north and west the potters were concerned with developing the circle style and producing more intricate shapes. The ox vase from Kourion (34) is a fine example decorated in black on a red ground (Black-on-Red ware). Others are in White Painted or Bichrome ware.

In this period many terracottas were dedicated in sanctuaries. The Cypriots believed that their dedications acted as substitutes for themselves as continuous worshippers. Others were buried in tombs. Techniques for the smaller pieces changed little, and handmade or 'snowman' figures were still popular, now often decorated in the bichrome technique *(see front cover)*. From some time in the eighth century BC the craftsmen began to make small terracottas in moulds having adopted the technique from the Near East. The smaller terracottas often have a trumpet-shaped body which may be either handmade or wheel-made with a handmade or moulded head (35).

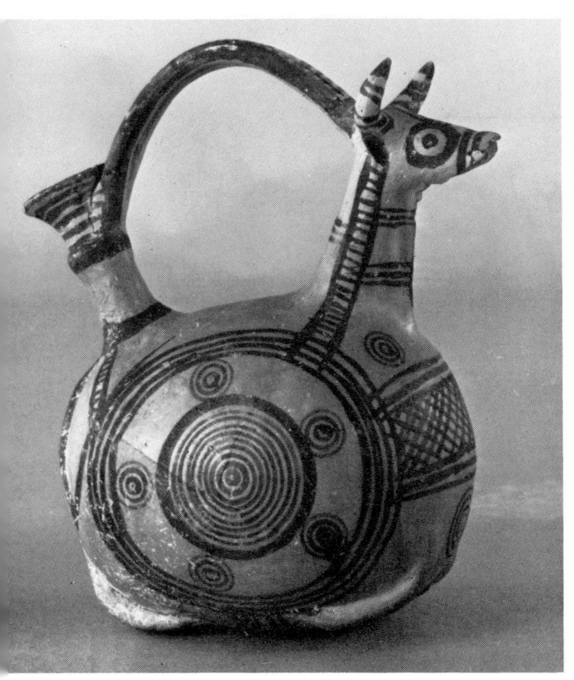

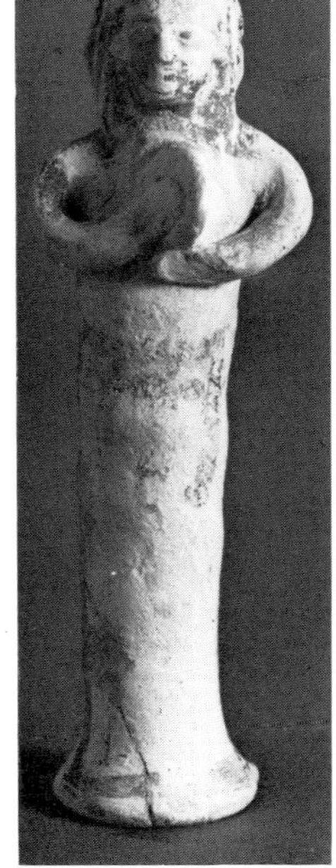

34 Ox-shaped flask (askos), Black-on-Red ware, from Kourion. 700–600 BC. *BMC Vases* C904. H.19.0 cm.

35 Terracotta tambourine player, from Larnaca. 700–600 BC. 66.1–1.235. H.17.8 cm.

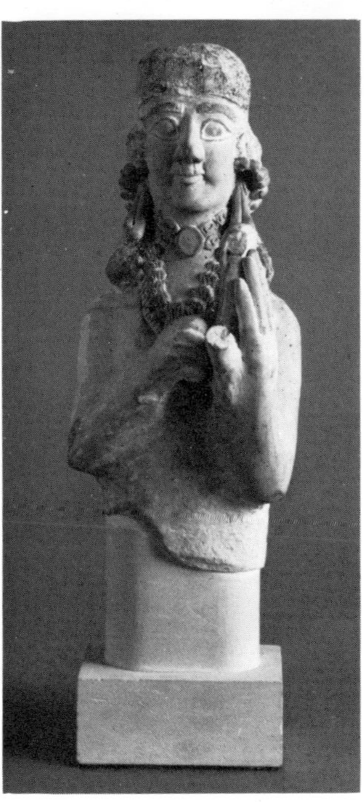

36 Terracotta harp player,
Neo-Cypriote style, from
Idalion. 600–550 BC.
73.3–20.87. H.30.7 cm.

Large-scale sculpture in limestone and terracotta began in the years of independence, around 670–660 BC. The terracottas were usually moulded or handmade in separate pieces and then joined together. Some remarkable colossal statues were produced in both media. The earlier, or Proto-Cypriote, style was essentially a local creation but does have affinities with sculpture from the Near East. Little attention is paid to the body, which is crudely modelled or flat and board-shaped. The heads are often triangular *(inside back cover)* or oval, but all have severe expressions, large eyes with feathered eyebrows and, for the men, long beards. Following contact with Egypt through the Greek trading post at Naucratis towards the end of the seventh century, the Neo-Cypriote style of the first half of the sixth century continued the Proto-Cypriote style, but now showed Egyptian and East Greek influence. Many of the Cypriote statues are similar to sculptures in the 'mixed style' from Naucratis, Rhodes and Samos, which show a mixture of oriental, Greek and Egyptian elements. The Cypriote sculptors still paid little attention to the body, which continued often to be board-shaped, but the hair may now be arranged in an Egyptian *klaft* (wig), the features are softer with a slight Greek 'Archaic' smile on the lips, and a variety of helmets derived from Near Eastern types are worn *(inside front cover)*. The women wear elaborate jewellery including ear-caps, ear-rings and necklaces, which can be paralleled by actual finds (36). They too may wear an Egyptian *klaft* but some have their hair arranged in elaborate spiral curls familiar from Syrian and Phoenician ivory work (36). Only a few statues are recorded in the true Cypro-Egyptian style, which are faithful copies of Egyptian models, and these must belong to the period of Egyptian rule.

It is the sculpture that particularly illustrates the effect of Cyprus's inclusion in the Persian empire. The pieces in the Archaic Cypro-Greek

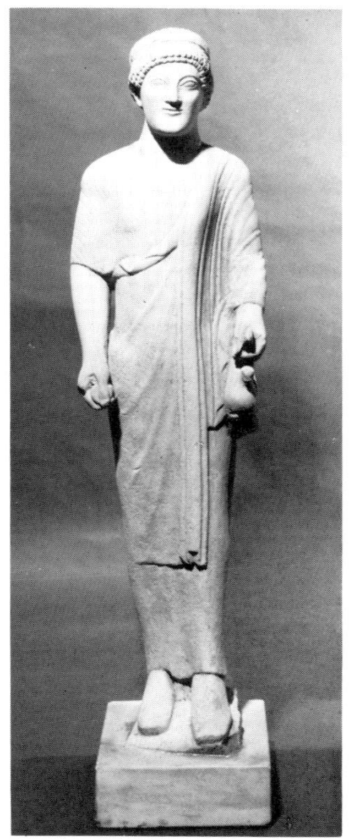

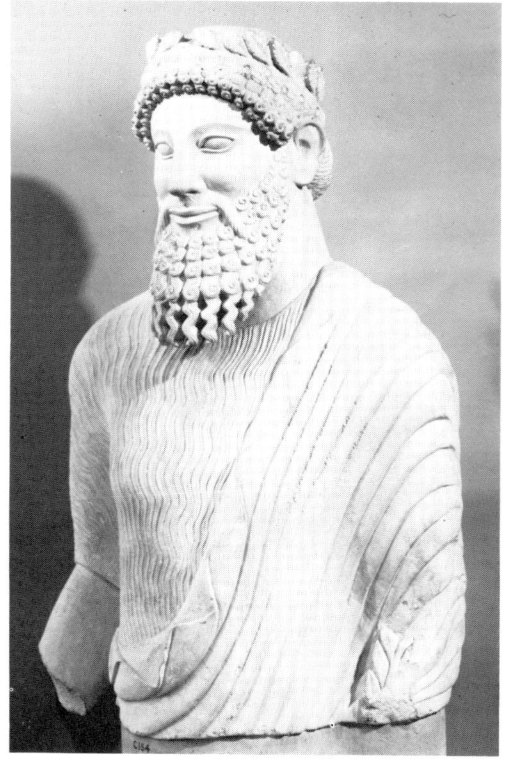

37 Limestone male statue, Archaic
Cypro-Greek style, from Idalion,
about 480 BC. *BMC Sculpture* C 131.
H.98.0 cm.

38 Limestone male statue, Archaic Cypro-Greek
style, from Idalion. 490–480 BC. *BMC Sculpture* C 154.
H.104.0 cm.

style of the later sixth century BC are similar to East Greek *kouroi*. They stand with the left leg advanced and the features are soft and round. The hair is usually short, secured by a wreath. Gone is the Egyptian *klaft* but the women still wear elaborate jewellery. The men's clothing, a *chiton* (tunic) partly covered by a *himation* (cloak), is a particular feature of the East Greek school (37, 38).

The stimulus provided by contacts with their neighbours, whether through trade or through submission to their rule, enabled the Cypriote artists to use their skills and produce work of their own with a definitely Cypriote quality. At this period models were not slavishly imitated but rather adapted to suit the Cypriote taste. The years of independence, during which the island continued its outside contacts, gave Cyprus a chance to develop distinct styles in pottery, sculpture and other media, while also playing a role in the transmission of goods and ideas above all to the Phoenician centres in the Western Mediterranean and the East Greek cities of Ionia. Internally the Cypriote cities grew powerful and were able to take a stand, albeit unsuccessful, against the Persian invasions in 498 BC. This defeat in the Ionian revolt was a turning point in Cypriote history and it was in the turmoil of Greek and Persian politics that Cyprus entered the Classical Period in about 475 BC.

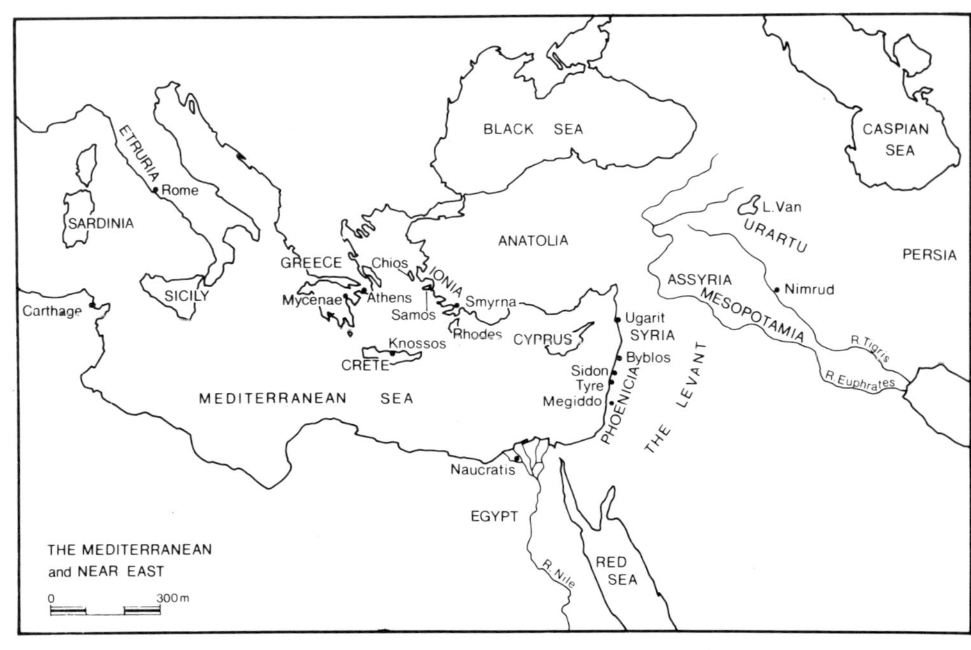

ETRURIA
Rome
SARDINIA
SICILY
Carthage
GREECE
Chios
Mycenae
Athens
Samos
Rhodes
Knossos
CRETE
IONIA
Smyrna
MEDITERRANEAN   SEA
BLACK   SEA
ANATOLIA
CYPRUS
Ugarit
SYRIA
Byblos
Sidon
Tyre
Megiddo
PHOENICIA
THE LEVANT
CASPIAN
SEA
L.Van
URARTU
PERSIA
ASSYRIA
Nimrud
MESOPOTAMIA
R Tigris
R Euphrates
Naucratis
EGYPT
R Nile
RED
SEA
THE MEDITERRANEAN
and NEAR EAST
0   300m

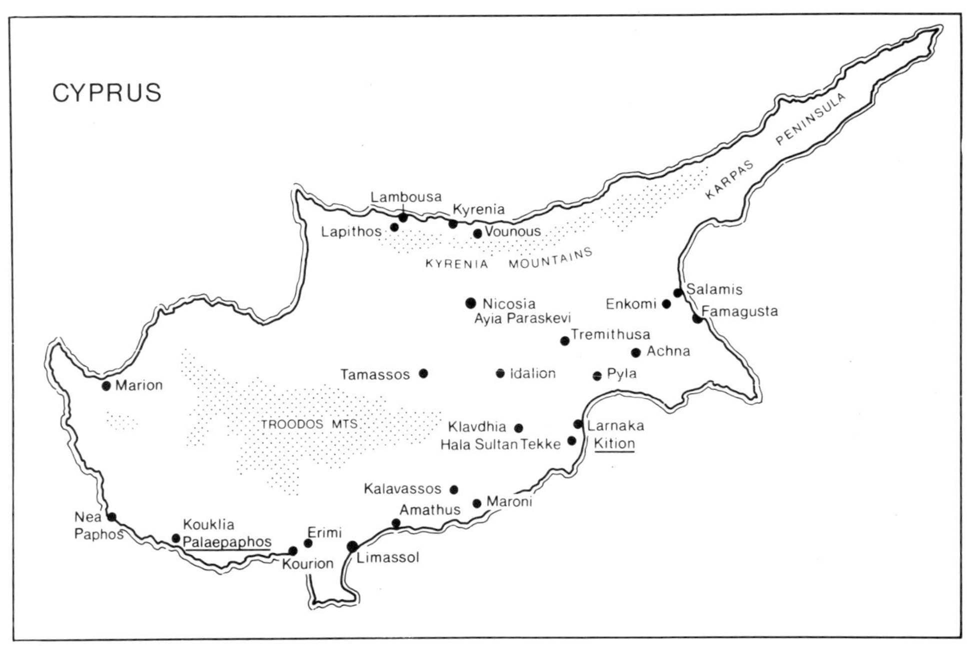

CYPRUS
Lambousa
Kyrenia
Lapithos
Vounous
KARPAS PENINSULA
KYRENIA MOUNTAINS
Nicosia
Ayia Paraskevi
Enkomi
Salamis
Famagusta
Tremithusa
Achna
Tamassos
Idalion
Pyla
Marion
TROODOS MTS
Klavdhia
Larnaka
Hala Sultan Tekke
Kition
Kalavassos
Maroni
Amathus
Nea
Paphos
Kouklia
Palaepaphos
Erimi
Kourion
Limassol

The Classical Period

Throughout the Classical Period Cyprus was poised between Greece and Persia. The failure of the Ionian revolt in 498 BC left Persia for a time firmly in control but twenty years later the Cypriote cities were freed by an allied Greek fleet, although Persia retained control over the sea. The Cypriote cities themselves were becoming divided in their loyalties and a major expedition against Cyprus was launched by the Greeks in 450/449 BC. The main pro-Persian strongholds, Marion, Salamis and Kition, were laid to siege. Marion was taken and a phil-Hellene placed on the throne. The allied fleet, however, sailed for home after the death of its commander without completing the operations. The Peace of Kallias in 448 BC left Cyprus once again firmly in Persian control, as the Greeks had agreed to give up their interests in the Eastern Mediterranean. There was now a general anti-Hellenic movement in the island and a desire to ban all things Greek, which lasted until Evagoras I ascended the throne of Salamis in 411 BC. He was openly pro-Hellenic and welcomed both Greek imports and immigrants. He gradually increased his control so that by 391 BC, with help from Athens and Egypt, he ruled over virtually the whole of Cyprus. However, Athenian support was finally lost when, under the peace of Antalcidas in 386 BC, the Athenians agreed to recognise Persian sovereignty over the cities of Asia and two islands including Cyprus in return for which all the East Greek cities would be autonomous apart from three which would belong to Athens as before. Although left with Egypt as his only ally, Evagoras decided to fight on against Persia. He was eventually defeated at the battle of Kition in 381 BC but he still negotiated a settlement by which he retained the throne of Salamis although he lost control over the rest of Cyprus. In the succeeding years the Cypriote cities fought among themselves and Persia fostered this civil unrest. Evagoras was murdered in about 365 BC and his successors, although weaker than himself, continued the struggle against Persia. In 351 BC the nine remaining city kingdoms joined with Phoenicia and Egypt in another revolt against Persia. This was suppressed and when besieged, perhaps not until about five years later, Salamis voluntarily submitted. The entire forces of Cyprus were therefore momentarily at Persia's disposal. However, the forces of Greece under Alexander the Great, King of Macedon, were gaining considerable successes against the Persian Empire. This led the Cypriots to change their allegiance by 330 BC. Thus Persian domination was finally brought to an end for ever and Cyprus became fully hellenised and part of the Greek world.

The turn of events and the continual fluctuation between Persian and Athenian domination made for an uneasy political situation in Cyprus. The cities, as we have seen, were divided in their loyalties, while Salamis emerged as a major power. Ties both commercially and culturally were now with mainland Greece and the Persian Empire. Attic (Athenian) rather than East Greek pottery dominated the Cypriote market and influence from Classical Greece is apparent in several media.

Cypriote sculpture in bronze, limestone and terracotta illustrates the contrast between the intentional imitations of Classical Greek models

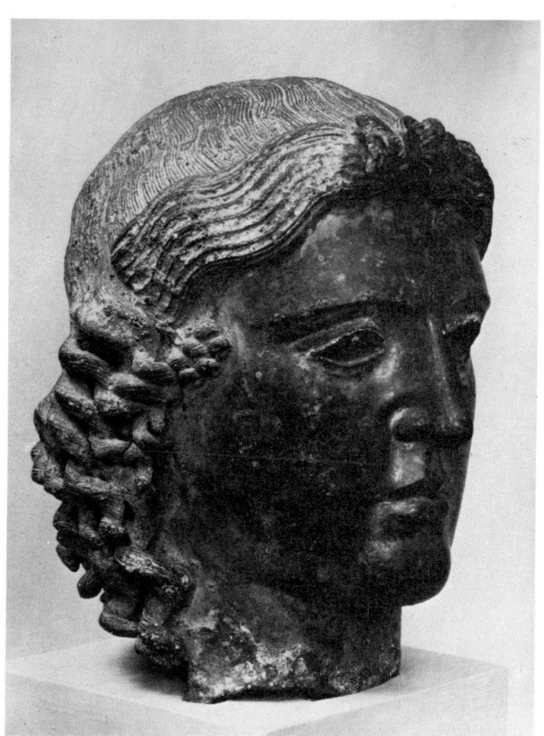 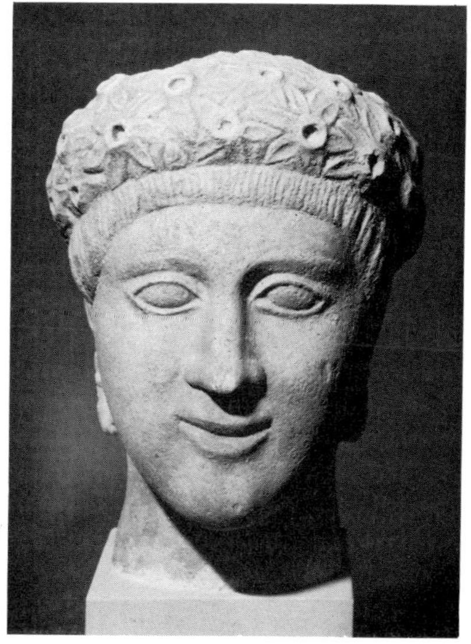

39 Bronze head of Apollo, the 'Chatsworth Head', from Tamassos. 470–460 BC. 1958.4–18.1. H.31.7 cm.

40 Limestone male head, Classical Cypro-Greek style, from Idalion, about 450 BC. *BMC Sculpture* C321. H.18.0 cm.

and local work in the native Cypriote styles that show little outside influence. The bronze head of Apollo from Tamassos (39), known as the Chatsworth Head from its long sojourn at Chatsworth House in Derbyshire, was cast hollow. Much of the hair was cast separately and attached; the eyes were originally inlaid. The body and limbs, which were melted down by the finders, were probably also cast separately and assembled at the foundry before export to Cyprus. It was no doubt made in Athens about 470–460 BC, the time of the 'severe style' in Greek sculpture. The artists had broken away from the rigid Archaic style and concentrated on representing the perfect human form, giving their works expression and movement. It was imports such as this that made a deep impression on Cypriote art of the period. Another work by a Cypriote sculptor who was closely following Attic models is a male head in the local limestone that was usual for Cypriote sculpture (40). It dates from the middle of the fifth century and is contemporary with works of famous Greek sculptors such as Pheidias and Polycleitus. With these it shares the feeling of idealism while the rendering of the hair is particularly Polycleitan. The rosettes of the wreath were originally inlaid. The bearded head (41) was made in the second quarter of the fifth century in the sub-Archaic Cypro-Greek style: this is simply a continuation of the Archaic style that directly preceded it (cf. 38). It gradually became stagnant and repetitive since no influence from outside was admitted. The later pieces are very poorly carved.

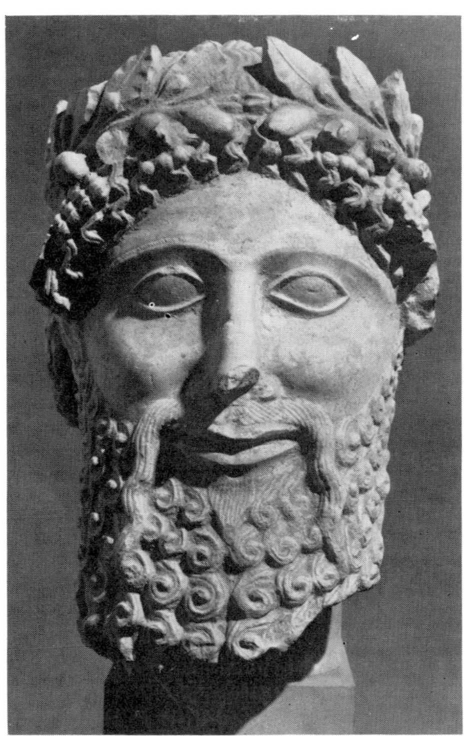

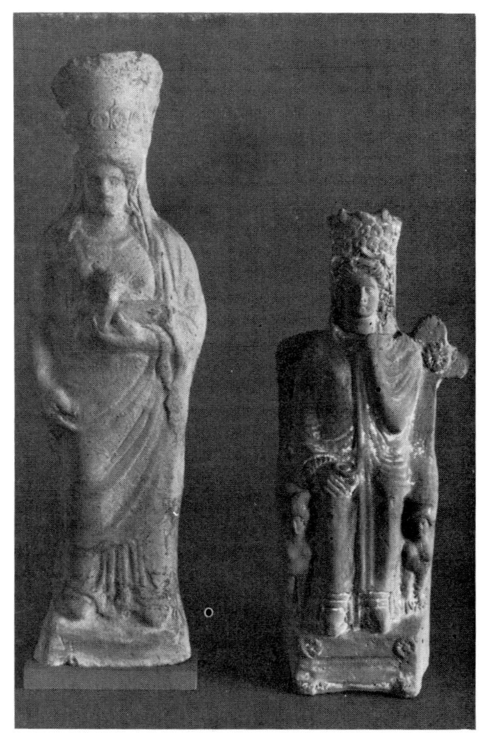

41 Limestone male head, Sub-Archaic Cypro-Greek style, probably from Pyla, about 450 BC. *BMC Sculpture* C 155. H.33.0 cm.

42 a) Terracotta offering bearer, from Larnaca. 400–300 BC. *BMC Terracottas* A 246. H.40.6 cm.
b) Terracotta seated goddess, from Achna. 400–300 BC. *BMC Terracottas* A 261. H.31.4 cm.

Some terracottas of the 'snowman' type were still made by hand but most were made in moulds. Like larger sculptures they usually follow Greek types. Greek dress consisting of a *chiton* (tunic) and *himation* (cloak) draped in the Greek fashion is worn by two examples of the fourth century BC. Both also have a tall *polos* (headdress) on the head. One (42a) stands with an offering held in front of the body in the left hand, a pose favoured by the Cypriots from the Archaic period. The other (42b) is seated on a throne supported by sphinxes. Of Near Eastern origin, the throne supported by sphinxes is found earlier than this in Cyprus, but here the sphinxes have short hair and sickle-shaped wings in the Greek manner. This figure is probably a goddess, either Aphrodite or Artemis, and it has been suggested that it represents the cult statue of Artemis as worshipped in a shrine established by Kitians in the Greek port at Peiraeus. Fine as it is it is certainly of Cypriote manufacture, although some figures in this style may have been made in imported Greek moulds.

Pottery tells a similar story. The same fabrics were employed, notably White Painted, Bichrome, Black-on-Red and Plain White; Bichrome Red, which adds ornament in supplementary white to the Black-on-Red ware, becomes popular and the white, originally used sparingly, is now as important as the black. Shapes are normally revised versions of the earlier types, which tend to become taller and slimmer. A fair amount of high quality Attic pottery was imported in the second half of the century, in particular by Marion under its phil-Hellenic king and then by Salamis. As a result some Greek ornaments were copied by Cypriote painters to decorate their own vessels. A favourite shape is a pitcher with a figure, usually a Greek *kore* (maiden) on the neck, pouring from a small jug which acts as the spout (43).

In the Classical Period Greek jewellery is in general known better from sites outside Greece than from Greece itself. Cyprus, South Russia, Thracian tombs at Duvanlij and parts of South Italy have produced a fair amount. Regional variations and preferences can be observed but it is difficult to identify different schools with certainty. Generally the archaic trends are continued but the workmanship is finer, although not reaching the standard of Greek jewellery of the seventh century. Filigree (wires soldered in patterns on a background) is used rather than granulation for decoration. Enamel is used for inlay (as on the griffins' necks, 44b) and is sometimes bordered by filigree (filigree enamel).

In fifth-century Cyprus acorn-shaped pendants with a gold cap were popular and illustration 44a shows one hanging from a necklace. Both the beads and the pendant are paralleled in South Russia and must come from the same, probably Greek, source. Gold-plated bronze was the medium in which the Cypriote jewellers often worked and spiral ear-

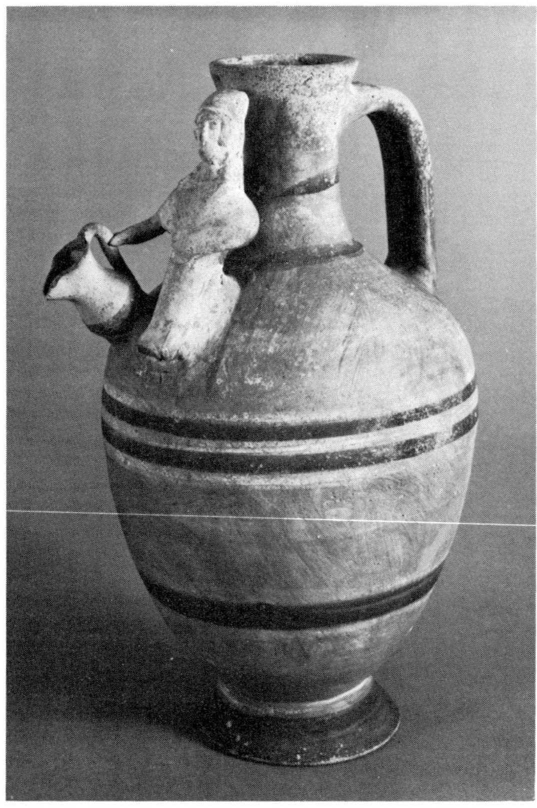

43 Pitcher, Bichrome Red ware, from Marion. 500–400 BC. *BMC Vases* C974. H.32.3 cm.

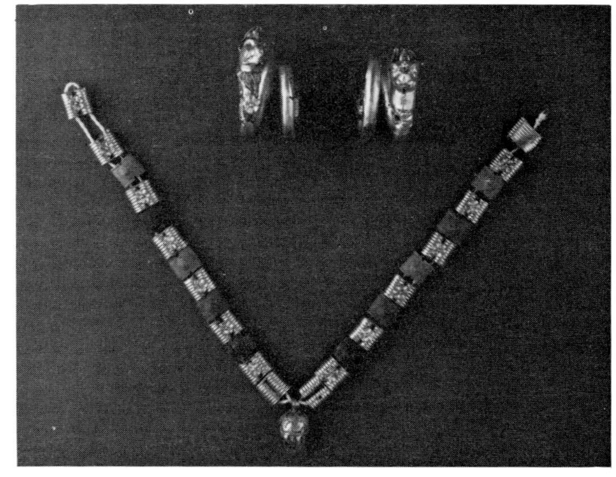

44 a) Gold necklace, from Amathus,
475–400 BC. *BMC Jewellery* 1957.
L.21.0 cm.
b) Pair of gold-plated bronze ear-rings,
from Amathus, 475–400 BC. *BMC
Jewellery* 1646–7. L.2.9, 2.8 cm.

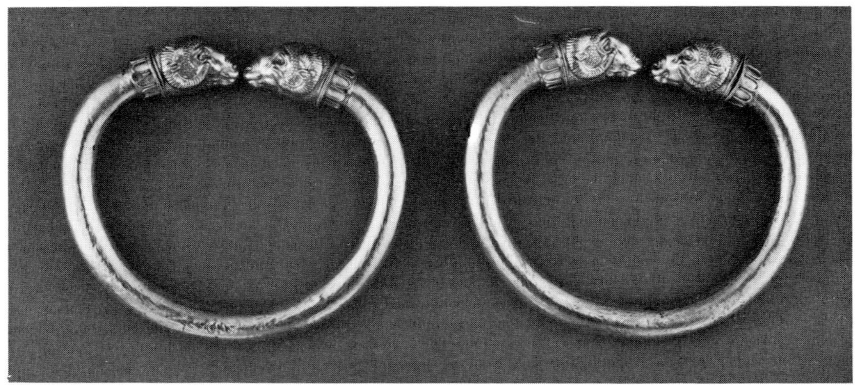

45 Pair of gold-plated bronze bracelets,
from Kourion. 475–400 BC. *BMC
Jewellery* 1985–6. D.8.4 cm.

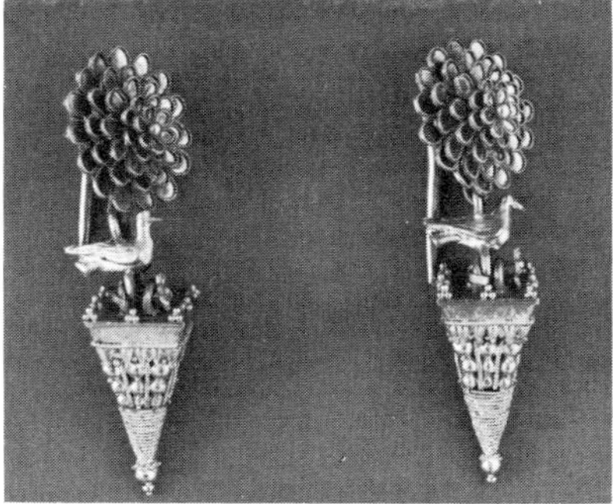

46 Pair of gold ear-rings. 350–300 BC.
BMC Jewellery 1666–7. L.5.2 cm.

rings terminating in heads, which are a particular favourite, may have
been made locally. In the same material are open-ended bracelets
terminating in animal heads (45). Originally Near Eastern, this type of
bracelet was copied and adapted by the Greeks, and it is interesting that
it is the Greek version that the Cypriots chose to imitate. Some bracelets
of the Achaemenid (Persian) type, with a depression in the hoop and
terminating in calves' or rams' heads have also been found in Cyprus.
Fourth-century BC jewellery can be very elaborate. Intricate pieces of
pure gold, like the ear-rings decorated with fine filigree (46), are of
Greek workmanship.

The continual warfare in Cyprus and the island's involvement in the struggles between Greece and Persia left the Cypriots with little real peacetime in which to develop and foster their own artistic ability. This is not to suggest that this period did not produce much of fine quality. However, while Archaic work is noted for its liveliness and originality, Classical Cypriote art is more directly dependent on its models. There are exceptions, particularly where relief sculpture is concerned, but on the whole the quality of art in this period depends on the extent of Greek influence. Where no new influence penetrates, the Archaic style continues, becoming gradually degenerate. This phenomenon is best observed in sculpture. We have noted some fine imports, but that the Cypriots themselves were capable of producing works of high quality is amply illustrated by some sculpture, terracottas and jewellery.

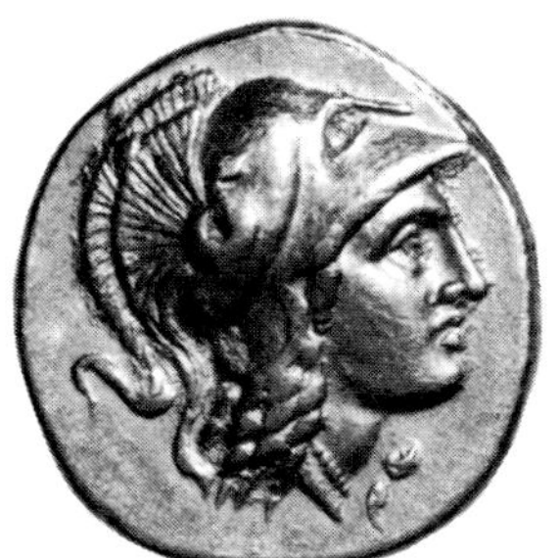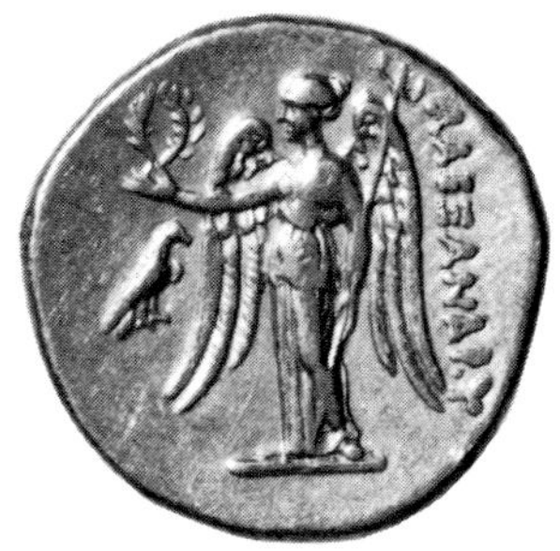

47 Gold stater of Alexander, minted at Salamis. About 325 BC. 1926.1–14.1. Twice actual size.

Hellenistic and Roman Cyprus

From Alexander the Great to Constantine the Great

DONALD M. BAILEY

The historical background

The Egyptian hold on the island of Cyprus was broken shortly after the middle of the sixth century BC, and thereafter, until the time of Alexander, the Persian Empire was nominally, and more often than not actually, in control.

After the victory of Alexander the Great over the Persians at the Battle of Issus in 333 BC, Cyprus transferred its allegiance to the Macedonian king, and contributed fleets of ships to various engagements. The island was still divided into separate kingdoms at this time, and Salamis continued to be the most powerful amongst them. However, the issue of independent coinage became a rarity, and coins of Alexander supplanted those of Cyprus (47).

As a source of copper, corn and ship-timber, Cyprus was always important, and became increasingly so after the death of Alexander in 323 BC was followed by the convoluted struggle for supremacy by his generals, of whom the most important were Antipater, Perdiccas, Polyperchon, Eumenes, Cassander, Ptolemy, Seleucus and Antigonus. In 321 Ptolemy I, the general who claimed Egypt as his share, allied himself with four Cypriote kings against Perdiccas. A few years later Ptolemy fought Antigonus for Cyprus and prevailed with the aid of Seleucus. Some Cypriote kings, in 312 BC, objected to Ptolemy's rule, and in 310 King Nicocreon of Salamis, and his royal household were forced to commit suicide after being accused by Ptolemy of disaffection. (A large tumulus near Enkomi, recently excavated, may be a monument to this event.) A peace between Ptolemy and Antigonus was arrived at in 309, but in 306 Demetrius Poliorcetes, son of Antigonus, landed in Cyprus and besieged Salamis. After winning a sea-battle with Ptolemy, Demetrius took possession of the entire island, and it was subject to Antigonus and Demetrius until 294, when Ptolemy retook it. Thereafter, except for a short period in the second century BC, Cyprus remained in Ptolemaic hands until its annexation by Rome. Thus for two and a half centuries it had comparative peace, although occasionally suffering attack by the Seleucid kings. The riches of the island were exploited for the benefit of the Egyptian kings, and the powers of the individual kingdoms were virtually suppressed (48). Paphos gradually became more powerful than Salamis. About 168 BC the island was conquered by Antiochus IV Epiphanes of Syria, but he was forced to

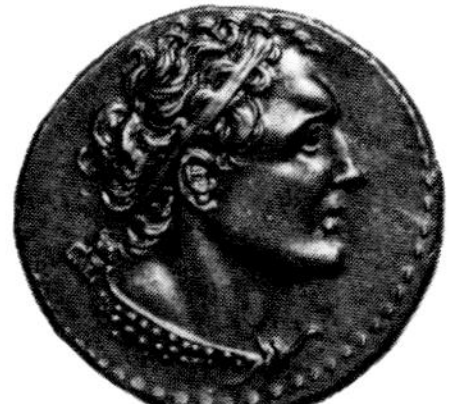
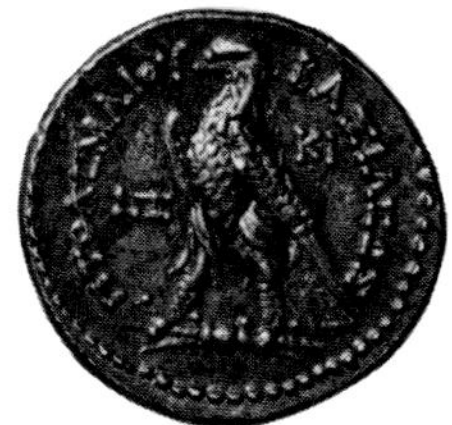

48 Silver tetradrachm of Ptolemy v, minted at Kition. 174 BC. *BMC Ptolemy* V 43.

withdraw by threats from Rome; thereafter Rome frequently intervened in the fortunes of Cyprus. About 80 BC Cyprus was severed from Egypt, but was placed by Rome under the rule of a member of the Ptolemy family. A law was passed in Rome in 58 BC, reducing the island to the condition of a province of Rome, Cato being appointed to oversee the transfer of power. Ptolemy, King of Cyprus, committed suicide, and Rome seized the island.

It suffered brutal and usurious exactions by individual Roman officials for their personal gain, although Cicero, sent there for a year in 51 BC appears to have been a figure of some probity. After 47 BC, Rome allowed the island to be governed by the remaining Ptolemies of Egypt, but on the death of Cleopatra VII in 30 BC Cyprus came finally to Rome. It was probably associated at first with the Roman Province of Cilicia, to the north, on the south coast of Asia Minor, but in 22 BC it became a Senatorial Province, to be governed henceforth by an ex-praetor (magistrate) with the title of Proconsul, until the reorganisation of the Empire by Diocletian and Constantine.

During the Roman Imperial period, Paphos remained the most important city in Cyprus until the fourth century AD, when Salamis-Constantia regained that distinction. Coins were minted in Cyprus from the time of Augustus, late in the first century BC at least until the reign of Caracalla (49). A major disaster affecting the island was the Jewish Revolt. There were large Jewish colonies on the island, probably originally established during the reign of Ptolemy I in the late fourth century BC. It was members of these communities who murdered Barnabas in Salamis, who thereafter became the patron saint of the island. During the years AD 115–117, Jews rose against the Roman establishment in Cyrene, Egypt and Cyprus. In the latter province, under their leader Artemion, Jews massacred thousands of the non-Jewish population of the island, and the city of Salamis is reputed to have been destroyed. Trajan's general Lusius Quietus dealt ruthlessly with the revolt, but it is not certain that he himself came to the island; it can be assumed that some of his army did. At first, after the suppression

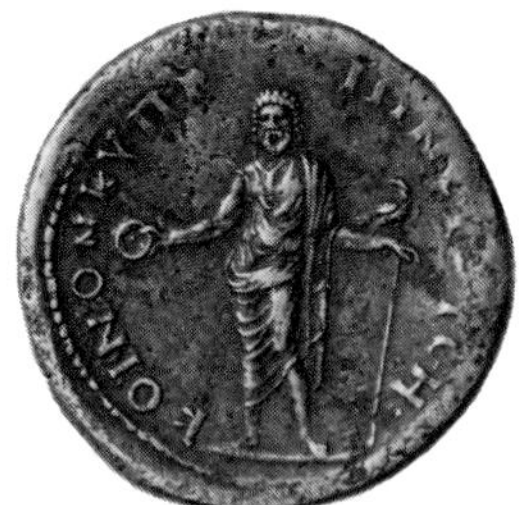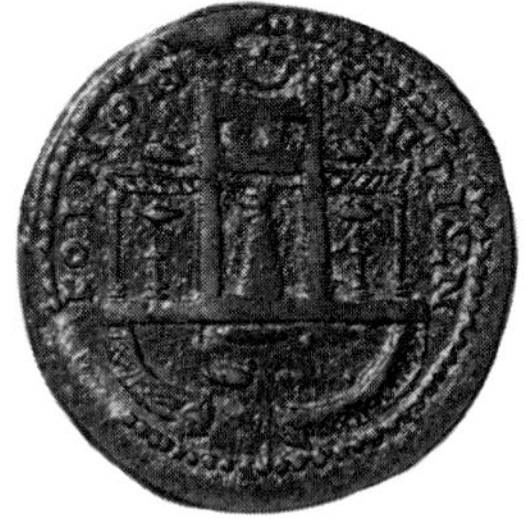

49 Roman coins of Vespasian (AD 69–79) and Caracalla (AD 198–217), showing Zeus Salaminios, and the Temple of Aphrodite at Paphos. *PCG* VIIIA 30; *BMC* 62.

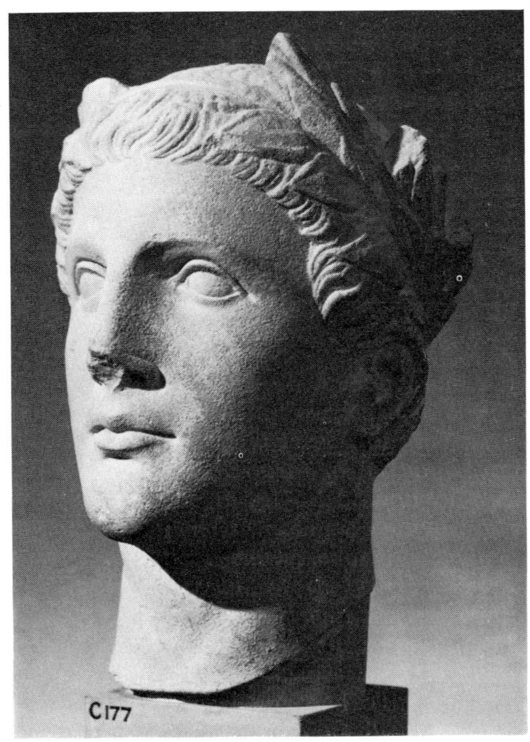

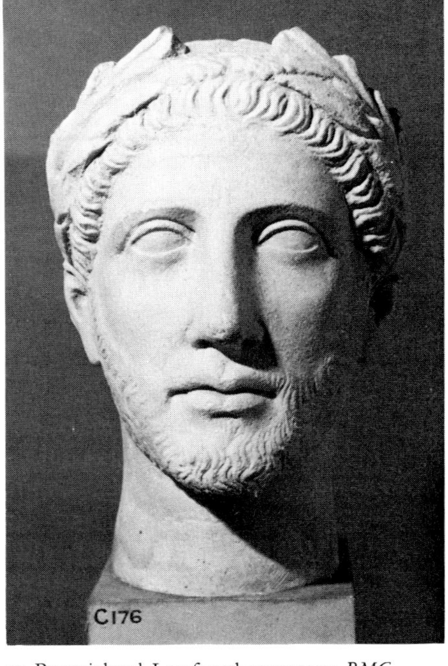

50 Portrait head. Late fourth century BC. *BMC Sculpture* C176. H.25.5 cm.

51 Portrait head of Demetrius Poliorcetes. Early fourth century BC. *BMC Sculpture* C177. H.35.0 cm.

of the revolt, no Jews were allowed on the island, but there is evidence to show that Jewish colonies there gradually built up again. Diocletian, in the later third century AD started to reorganise the Empire, a process continued by Constantine, and the Roman world was divided into dioceses; Cyprus was in the Orient Diocese, which included Libya, Egypt, Arabia, Mesopotamia, the Levant and Southern Asia Minor, although Libya and Egypt eventually became a separate diocese. Cyprus was governed by a *consularis, vir clarissimus*.

Except for the usurious exactions of the late Republic, the Jewish Revolt and a brief incursion by Gothic tribes in AD 269, the lot of Cyprus under Roman rule was relatively happy, particularly during Severan times, in the later second century and early third, when relations between Cyprus and the imperial family were apparently close. However, the transition to the rule of Byzantium was marred by drought and famine in the earlier fourth century and by several seismic disturbances at different times, culminating in the almost complete destruction of Salamis in AD 342. It was rebuilt, much reduced, and renamed Constantia.

Hellenistic and Roman Art

The fine and applied arts of Hellenistic and Roman Cyprus are not particularly well represented in the collections of the British Museum, especially if they are compared with the rich Bronze Age material, and the flamboyant decorative products of the Iron Age, described earlier in this book. In the third and second centuries BC, sculptors throughout the Eastern Mediterranean, working for and under the brilliant courts of the Hellenistic kings, basing their skills and knowledge on the great sculptors of the fifth and fourth centuries, reached new peaks of ability in representational sculpture. Although some centres were more skilful than others (Pergamon for example), the general styles of sculpture were fairly uniform over the entire Greek East, a state of affairs brought about by the ready emigration of sculptors and the patronage of the Hellenistic kings. Cyprus did not escape this ambience of high quality sameness, as is indicated by some of the fine marble sculpture found in the island, but the necessary use of local limestone by many of the native sculptors caused an insidious Cypriote effect to creep into their products: the actual material and its limitations dictated to a large extent the results obtained. Another factor which influenced the appearance of much of the surviving local sculpture of the Hellenistic Period is the reason for its production: most pieces were made as votive offerings at shrines, not as objects of decorative or monumental character. In this they followed a long tradition of religious dedication, descended as they are from such predecessors as the Archaic terracotta sculptures found in profusion in sanctuaries like that of Ayia Irini. These holy places must have presented an extraordinary sight, much of them open to the sky and packed with limestone and bronze sculptures and terracotta figures, of all sizes and complexity, from tiny clay votives to colossal stone statues, of many dates and periods. Idalion, for example, the site from which ills. 50–5 come, was excavated in a rough and ready fashion in 1868, and consisted of a few structures around a courtyard, and had more than a thousand votive figures in the excavated area, a hundred of which were over life-size. The bronze statues had largely disappeared, to be melted down, but the damaged remains of limestone sculptures remained in massed profusion. The shrine, possibly that of a Phoenician Apollo, dates back at least to the seventh century BC and some of the really colossal sculpture is of the Archaic Period. It remained in use well into the Hellenistic Period, perhaps declining during the early years of the second century BC.

It has been argued, with some degree of plausibility, that many of the votive figures of the Hellenistic Period have their facial features based upon portrait sculptures of the rulers of the island. Certainly, the late-fourth-century bearded and wreathed head from Idalion in ill. 50, broken from a statue of rather more than life-size, has every appearance of being a portrait, and Nicocreon, King of Salamis has been suggested. It was he, as mentioned earlier, who together with his family, committed suicide in 310 BC, after a charge of disaffection by Ptolemy I. Demetrius Poliorcetes, son of Antigonus I, ruler of Asia, conquered Cyprus in 306 BC and was dislodged by Ptolemy in 294. His portrait may be recognised in ill. 51, from a colossal votive statue found at Idalion. Also reminiscent

53 Votive statue of a child, wearing festive clothing and jewellery. Late fourth century BC. *BMC Sculpture* C 164. H.41.0 cm.

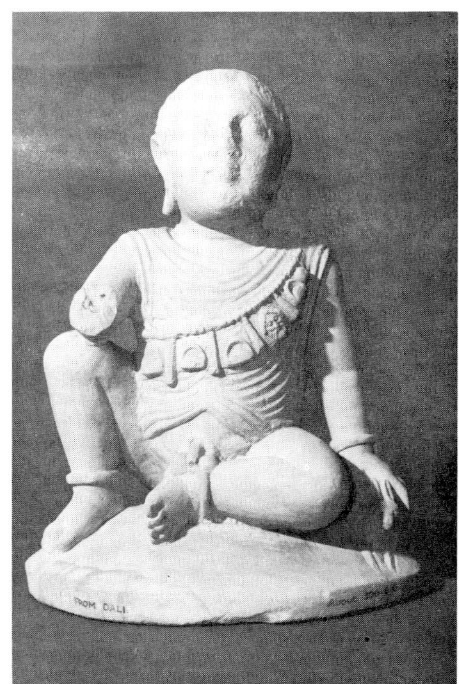

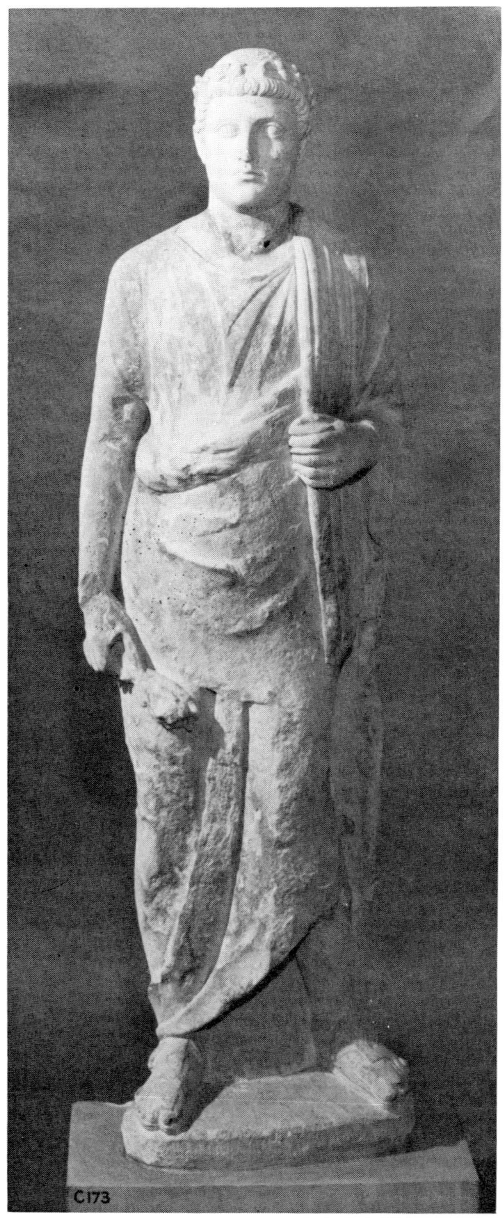

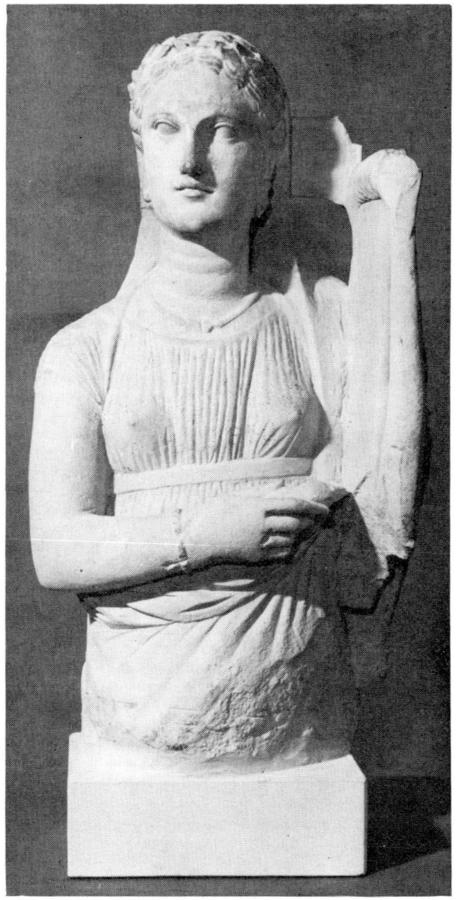

52 Votive statue. About 300 BC. *BMC Sculpture* C 173. H.116.0 cm.

54 Votive statue of a lyre-player. Early third century BC. *BMC Sculpture* C 352. H.55.5 cm.

of Demetrius is the small statue from this site shown in ill. 52.

Representations of small boys, perhaps made to commemorate their first dedication of an offering at the shrine, are a common feature of holy places in Cyprus during the fourth and later centuries. Illustration 53 shows such a child, wearing a short tunic, ear-rings, anklets, bracelets, and a sash of jewellery (probably hairlooms), seated holding the hare or rabbit he has offered to the god at Idalion. It dates to the end of the fourth century BC and has been painted in bright colours, the details of the jewellery picked out in red and yellow, and the flesh and rabbit painted red.

Women lyre-players form a large group of votive statues from Cypriote shrines, and a rather fine example of nearly life-size comes from Idalion (54). Unfortunately the lower part of the figure is lost. The face is probably based upon portrait statues of Berenike I, wife of Ptolemy I, and the figure is likely to be of the first quarter of the third century BC. Details are picked out in black, yellow and red paint.

Although it has been suggested that the shrine at Idalion was still the recipient of official votive statues based upon rulers until well into Roman times, and that ill. 55 is meant to be a portrait of Augustus, this

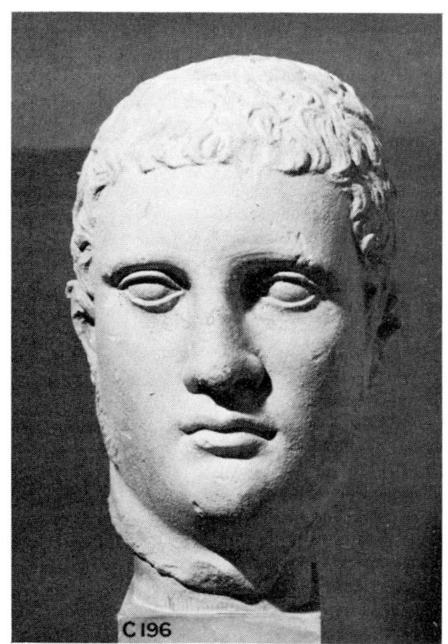

55 Portrait head. Third century BC.
BMC Sculpture C 196. H.27.0 cm.

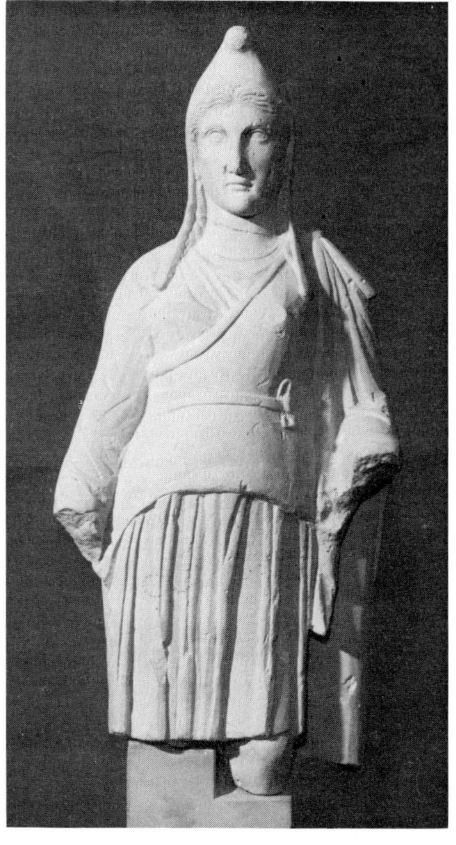

56 Figure of Artemis Bendis. Third century BC.
BMC Sculpture C 382. H.51.0 cm.

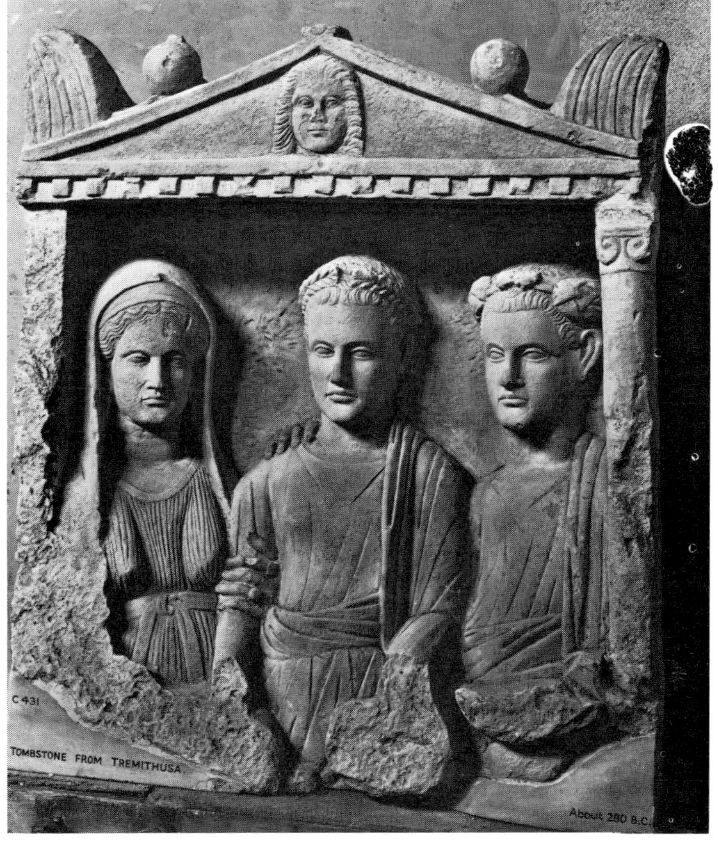

57 Grave relief: deceased young man with his parents. First half of the third century BC. *BMC Sculpture* C 382. H. 51.0 cm.

does not seem likely and a third century BC portrait is more probable, possibly Ptolemy III, of the third quarter of that century.

The bulk of the Museum's finer Cypriote sculpture came from the Apollo sanctuary at Idalion, but some good pieces came from elsewhere, a few, as ill. 56, from a site at Pyla, of which few details are known, but which may have also been dedicated to a local form of Apollo. Illustration 56 shows a large statuette of Artemis Bendis, wearing a short tunic and a Persian cap; it is of the third century BC.

Some of the surviving Cypriote sculpture of the Hellenistic Period had functions other than votive offerings, and ill. 57 has the upper part of a grave-relief, similar to those which were such a feature of fourth-century cemeteries in Athens. Within a shrine three figures stand, in the centre the deceased, a young man, flanked by two elderly people, presumably his mother and father. The figures are all based upon types of votive statues, the more familiar products of the Cypriote sculptors, here rendered in relief and side-by-side. It is competent work of the first half of the third century BC.

Marble, presumably because most of it had to be imported, and was therefore expensive, is less commonly found than limestone as a medium for the production of sculpture in Cyprus. Marble sculptures tended to be more of a monumental or decorative character than limestone, and

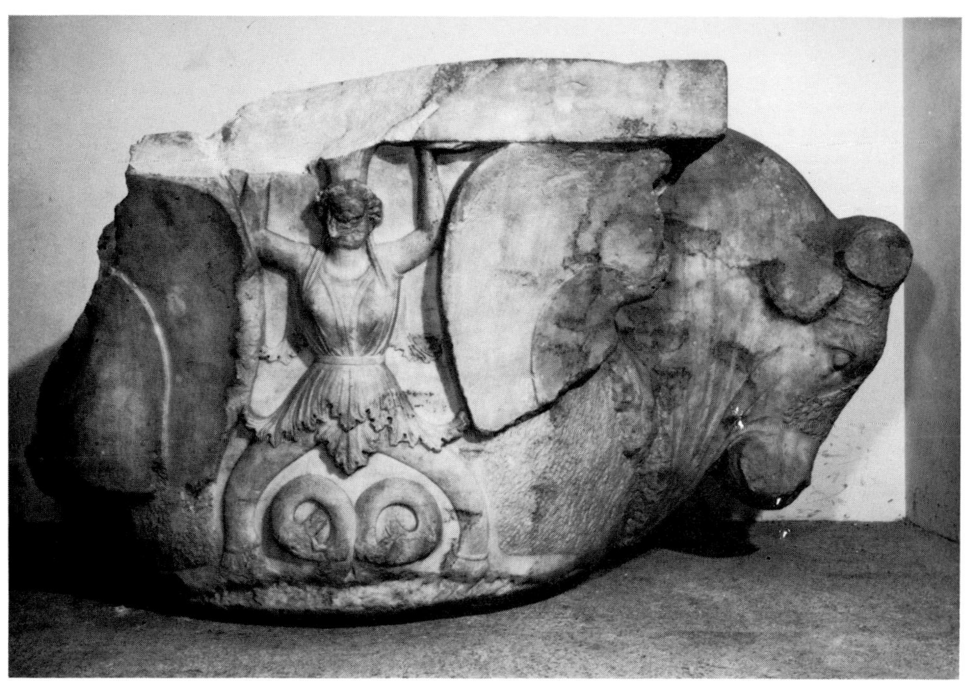

58 Column capital, with bulls' heads and caryatid figure. Probably early third century BC. *BMC Sculpture* 1510. H.96.0 cm.

the former material is not often found amongst the host of statuary dedicated at sanctuaries. This state of affairs is the more evident as most surviving marble sculpture is of the Roman period, by which time many of the small open-air shrines like that at Idalion had fallen out of use and the practice of devoting stone figures had been largely discontinued. However, some fine quality marble sculptures of the Hellenistic Age have been found, such as the Aphrodite from Soloi in Nicosia Museum, and marble was also used in the construction of important buildings, as the surviving column-capital shown in ill. 58 indicates. It was found in the Agora at Salamis, with little or no sign of the structure it once adorned. It is of most unusual design, with two bulls' heads and a part human, part plant caryatid figure between them. It has been argued that it is of the early third century, of the time when Demetrius Poliorcetes governed the island, and this is very possible. Alternatively, there is no reason on stylistic grounds why it should not belong to the very early Roman Empire, in the later first century BC or the early first century AD.

Two marble sculptures of the Roman period are illustrated. Illustration 59 is a fine portrait head of early Imperial date, possibly representing the Emperor Augustus. It is said to have been found in Cyprus, but no closer provenence was given. Salamis was a large and prosperous city in the second century AD, and a great deal of marble sculpture has been found there in the excavations of the post-war years. Much of this sculpture must have been imported from production centres in the Greek East, rather than made in the island. The woman's head in ill. 60 is probably not a portrait, but an idealised head with a hairstyle of the period of Trajan or Hadrian. It may well have been part of a statue of Demeter- or Tyche-type which adorned a large public building, such as the Gymnasium at Salamis.

During the Severan period, late in the second century and early in the third, the island continued prosperous and indeed there is some evidence that building programmes increased. One of the finest colossal Roman bronzes surviving from antiquity is the statue of Septimius Severus found at Kythrea and now in Nicosia Museum. Such bronze figures were, perhaps, the highest manifestation of the sculptor's art, but were particularly vulnerable to economic necessity, the large majority terminating their existence in the melting-pot. This Museum has no large-scale Hellenistic and Roman bronze figures from Cyprus, and very few small statuettes, and these of no great interest. After Severan times, from about the second quarter of the third century AD, the importation of sculpture on a large scale ceased, and not much was produced on the island.

Terracotta figures were produced in Cyprus in huge numbers for votive reasons from the Archaic Period onwards, and most exhibit a distinctive Cypriote appearance, easily distinguished from coroplastic

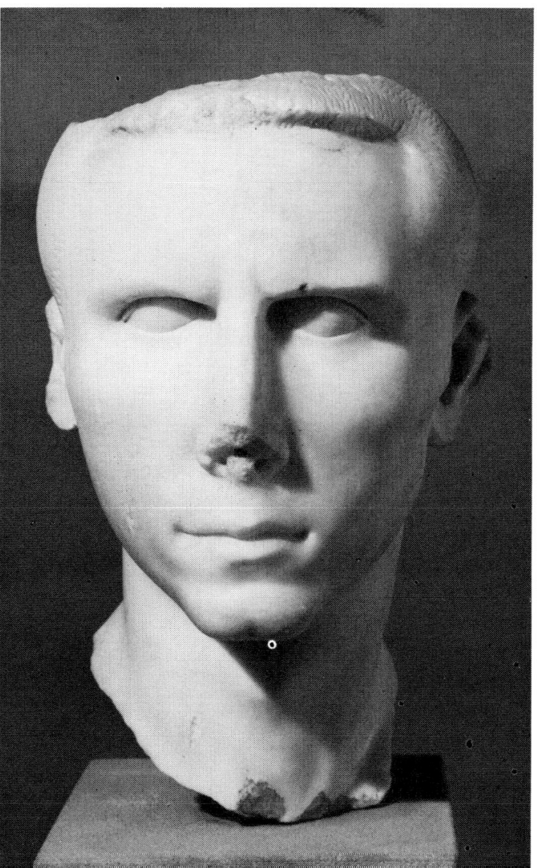

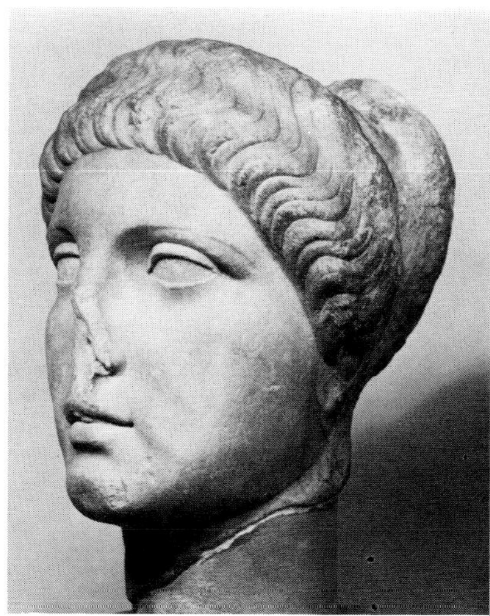

59 Portrait head of the Emperor Augustus. Late first century BC or early first century AD. *BMC Sculpture* 1879*. H.38.5 cm.

60 Woman's head. Second century AD. *BMC Sculpture* 1992. H.22.5 cm.

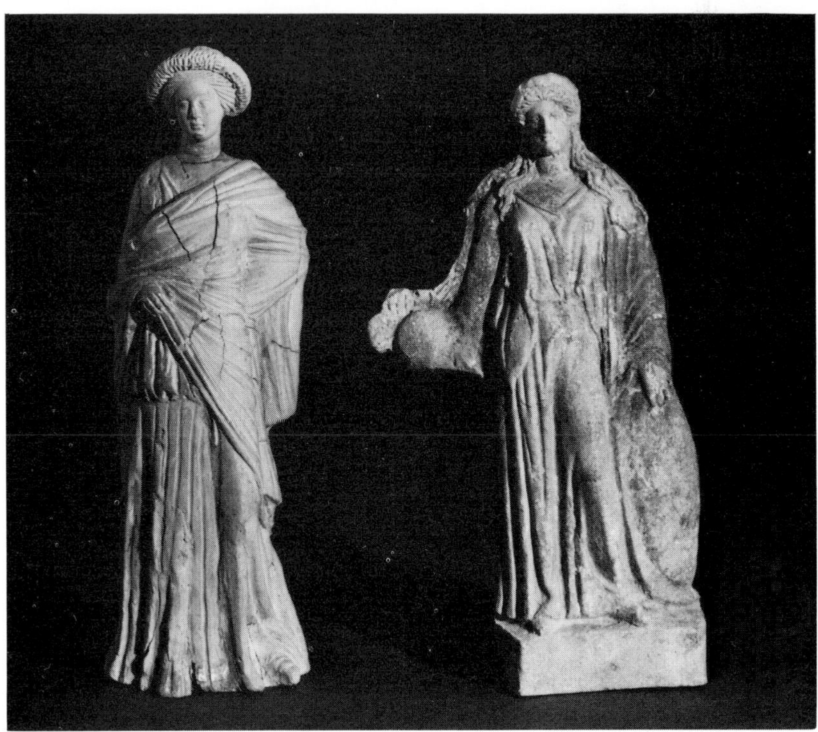

61 Terracotta figures: a girl, third century BC, and Athena, second or first century BC.
BMC Terracottas A 410. H.21.0 cm; *BMC Terracottas* A 423. H.20.3 cm.

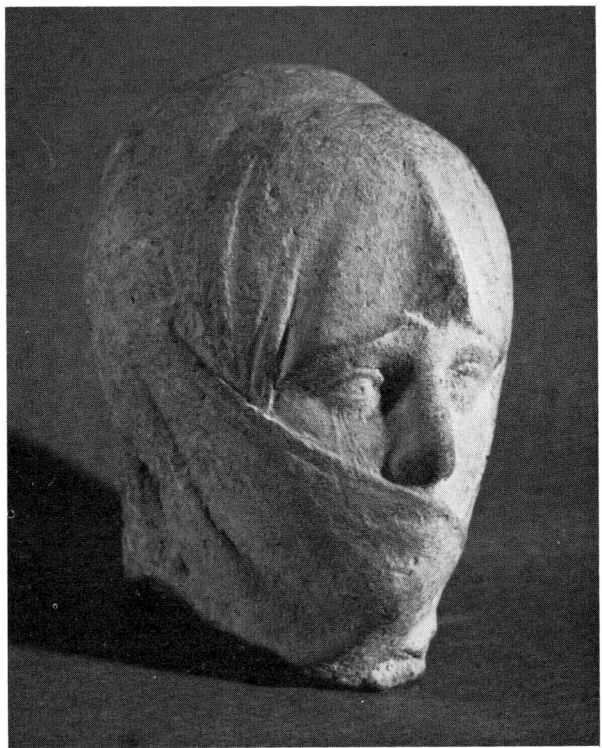

62 Terracotta head of a woman. Late fourth
century BC. *BMC Terracottas* A 394. H.4.1 cm.

products from other ancient sources. However, in Hellenistic times many decorative figures were produced on the island which are no different in appearance from contemporary products from Greece and Asia Minor. Two examples of these are illustrated here (61), a girl, attractively modelled and heavily draped, of the third century BC, found in a tomb at Amathus, and a figure of the goddess Athena, probably of the second or first century BC, from Salamis. An attractive veiled head of a woman, with her mouth and chin well-rendered beneath the cloth of the veil, is probably based upon early examples of the Tanagra style, of the later fourth century BC; many examples of this Cypriote version have been found on the island, and they represent the work of the Hellenistic Cypriote coroplast at its most sensitive (62).

Pottery is the most ubiquitous of ancient artefacts, and complete vessels are found in vast numbers in the tombs of Cyprus. Earlier chapters of this book have emphasised the versatility, ingenuity and flamboyancy of the native potter-craftsmen. In Hellenistic and Roman times, influences from abroad are the main characteristics of Cypriote pottery, at least as far as the tablewares are concerned (63, 64). The squat wine-jug with the fish decoration, and the deep cup (63), both have their origins in Greek lands, the latter in the Greek mainland and southern Italy, the former in Cyrenaica; both are of the third century BC. The small

63 Group of Hellenistic pottery and glass: glass amphoriskos, first century BC. 1894.11–1.325. H.10.5 cm; deep drinking cup, third century BC. *BMC Vases* C940. H.17.7 cm; Grey ware drinking cup, second century BC. 1881.8–24.70; clay lamp, third century BC. *BMC Lamps* Q500. L.8.4 cm; wine-jug decorated with fishes, third century BC. 1881.8–24.50. H.17.8 cm.

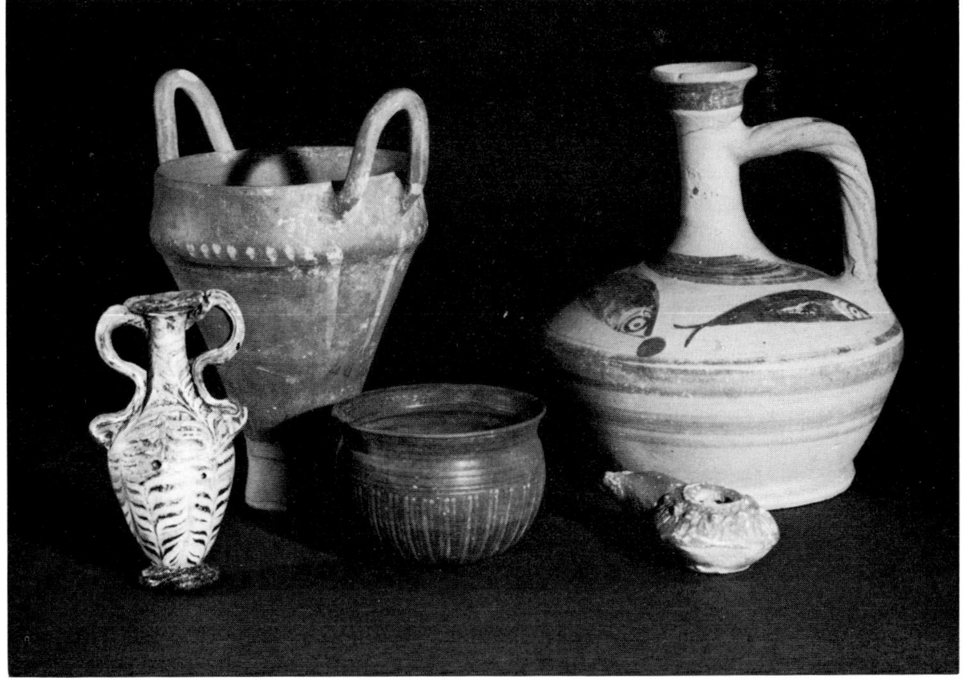

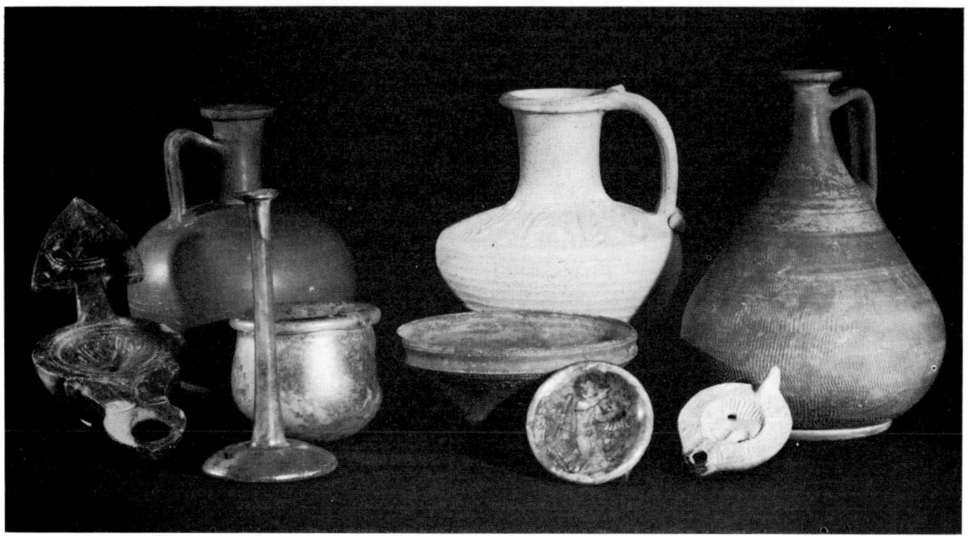

64 Group of Roman pottery and glass: clay lamp, first century AD. *BMC Lamps* 809. L.25.5 cm; Red ware wine-jug, second century AD. 1908.4–11.10. H.19.5 cm; glass bottle, late first or early second century AD. 1896.2–1.298, H.16.0 cm; glass bowl with painted lid, late first or early second century AD. 1872.7–26.6. H.7.8 cm; Red ware drinking-cup, late first century BC or early first century AD. 1876.9–9.40. H.6.8 cm; White ware jug with 'cut-glass' decoration, Roman Period. 1884.12–10.258. H.21.6 cm; glass lid, painted with figure of Eros, late first or early second century AD. 1888.11–12.1. D.7.4 cm; clay lamp, third-fourth century AD. 1973.4–15.1. L.8.9 cm; Red ware wine-jug, second century AD. 1876.9–9.47. H.22.8 cm.

grey drinking-cup with vertical ribbing may not be of Cypriote manufacture, but was found in Cyprus; a second-century date is likely. Two of the wine-jugs in ill. 64, and the cup in the centre, are of red wares, similar to the late Hellenistic and Roman products of Pergamon and other Eastern Greek centres, but they were quite probably made in Cyprus. The cup is of the late first century BC or early first century AD, and the jugs are of the second century AD. The coarseware jug with the 'cut-glass' decoration, from Salamis, is of the Roman period but not closely datable.

Although no glassworks have been scientifically excavated in the island, the existence of shapes which are peculiar to Cyprus shows that glass was manufactured there. The variegated amphoriskos from Amathus in ill. 63 is late Hellenistic, and was made round a core of removable material; there is little reason to doubt that it was made in Cyprus. Following the invention of glass-blowing in early Roman Imperial times there was a huge increase in the use of this material for tablewares, etc., and large glassworks were established in many parts of the Empire. The tall oil or perfume bottle in ill. 64 was free-blown in clear glass. Its shape, with an exaggerated low, wide body, is known from elsewhere, but seems to be especially prevalent in Cyprus. This example from a Roman tomb at Kourion is of late first-century or early second-century date. Other blown glass vessels of Cypriote manufacture include a particular type of lidded container, the lids often decorated with a scene painted on the inside, but meant to be seen through the glass from the outside. Both the lidded container and the separate lid shown in ill. 64 are decorated in this way; each has a figure of Eros painted on it. They are of late first- or second-century date; the lid was found in a tomb near the Aphrodite Temple at Paphos.

Lamps are a necessity of civilised life, and they were made and used in countless thousands in Mediterranean lands during Classical times. These everyday objects were often highly decorated. During the Hellenistic and Roman Periods the vast majority of pottery lamps were mass-produced from moulds. In Cyprus, lamps were manufactured on a huge scale. In ill. 63 is a Hellenistic lamp with formal floral patterning on the shoulder. It was made in the third century BC and was found in a tomb at Kourion. Two Roman lamps are shown in ill. 64, a large lamp of the first century AD, from Salamis, with a rosette decorating its top and a scene of Odysseus tied to the mast on its handle-ornament, and a more normal-sized lamp, of the third–fourth century AD, decorated with a lion on a rosette background, and signed by the Cypriote lampmaker Sphyridonos.

Not since the Late Bronze Age was there as much gold in the Greek Eastern Mediterranean as that which became available after Alexander's conquest of the Persian Empire, and this state of affairs is reflected in the

65 Group of Hellenistic and Roman jewellery: pair of ear-rings, third century BC. *BMC Jewellery* 1728–9. D. 2.2 cm; rosettes, stars and a pendant, from a necklace, fourth century BC. *BMC Jewellery* 2053–7. W.1.2 cm, 1.3 cm, H.7.3cm respectively; decorative pin, third century BC. *BMC Jewellery* 1999. L.17.8 cm; gold and garnet necklace, second or third century AD. *BMC Jewellery* 2710. L.43.2 cm; pair of gold and blue-glass ear-rings, second or third century AD. *BMC Jewellery* 2407–8. H.2.9 cm; gold ear-rings with intaglio gem settings, first or second century AD. *BMC Jewellery* 2677–8; *BMC Gems* 2779, 2795. H.3.0 cm.

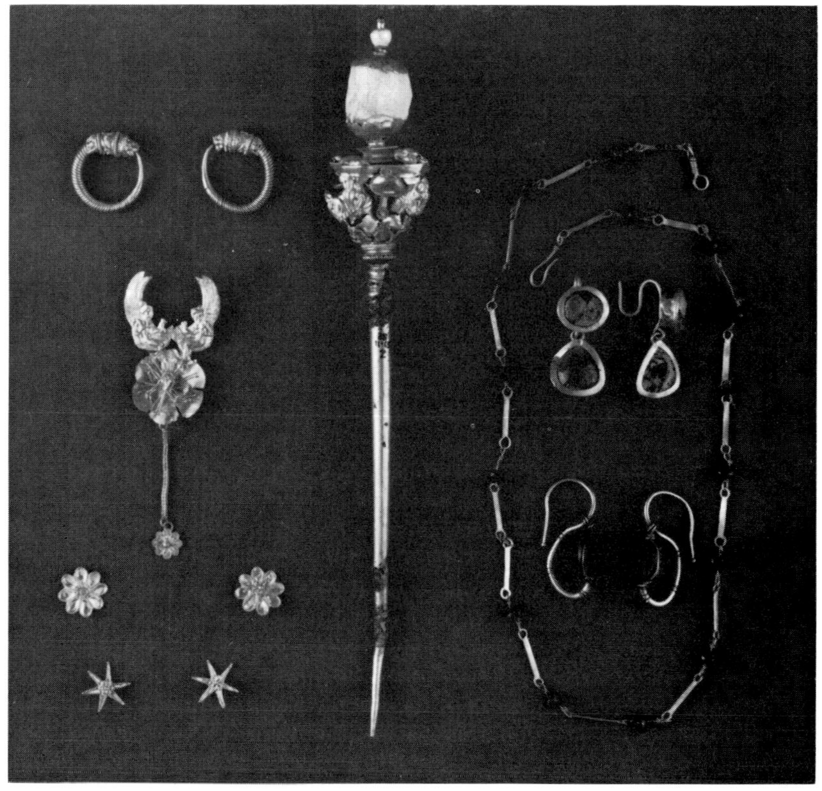

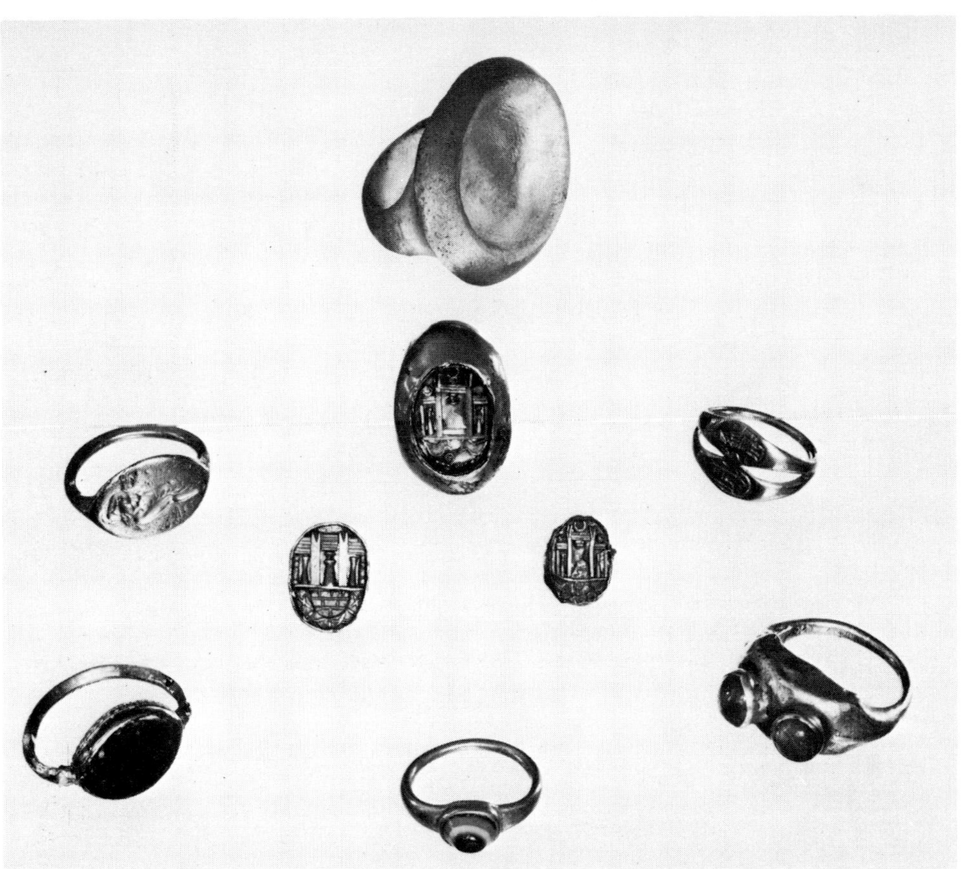

66 Group of Hellenistic and Roman finger-rings: glass ring, third century BC. *BMC Finger-rings*
1563.D.3.8 cm; gold ring with engraved bezel, fourth century BC. *BMC Finger-rings* 61.D.2 cm; gold
ring-setting showing the Temple of A-hrodite at Paphos, second-third century AD. *BMC Finger-rings* 1641.L.1.5 cm; gold ring with Aphrodite Temple, second-third century AD. *BMC Finger-rings*
253.D.2.4 cm; gold ring-setting with Aphrodite Temple, second-third century AD. *BMC Finger-rings*
1640.L.1.2 cm; gold ring with double engraved bezel, second-third century AD. *BMC Finger-rings*
175.D.1.9 cm; gilded bronze ring with glass setting, fourth century BC. *BMC Finger-rings* 1242.D.
2.3 cm; gold ring with sardonyx setting, second-third century AD. *BMC Finger-rings* 811.D.1.8 cm;
gold ring with two sapphire settings, third-fourth century AD. *BMC Finger-rings* 851.D.2.3 cm.

tombs of Cyprus. Personal jewellery became plentiful, and this remained
the case throughout the Hellenistic Period and well into the Roman
Imperial Period. Despite ancient and modern tomb-robbing many fine
pieces survive. It is not possible to say which of those pieces which
remain were imported by the island and which were made there, but it
seems likely that much was produced by jewellers on the island, working
within the current fashionable repertoires. Some of the motifs, such as
the representations of the Aphrodite Shrine at Paphos (four examples in
ill. 66) probably indicate local manufacture. Ear-rings are plentiful in
both Hellenistic and Roman times, and the lion-headed examples from
Kourion in ill. 65 are indistinguishable from examples found all over the
Hellenistic world in the third century BC, the shape continuing in fashion
long after this; the gaudy paste settings of the Roman ear-rings in the
same illustration are more to the Roman taste. Illustration 65 also has
elements from an exquisite necklace, found at Marion, composed of
rosettes and stars and a central pendant ornamented with figures of Eros

and rosettes; it is probably of the later fourth century BC. A Roman gold and garnet necklace of the second or third centuries AD is included. The striking gilt bronze, gold and glass-paste pin in the centre of the illustration, with a decorative column capital, is Hellenistic of the third century BC. It was found on the site of the Temple of Aphrodite at Paphos, and was probably a votive gift at that shrine. Hellenistic finger-rings illustrated include two from Kourion, one in gold with an engraved design of a reclining woman, another of gilded bronze with a green glass setting: this type, with oval bezels, probably was made for much of the fourth century BC. The large glass ring at the top of the illustration (66) is apparently a Cypriote Hellenistic speciality; it probably dates to the third century BC. In Roman times, representations of the Aphrodite Temple at Paphos are found both on coins (49) and on jewellery. Two rings and two ring-bezels in gold with this device are shown in ill. 66. They probably all date to Antonine or Severan times (second to early third century AD); the double-ring has also a representation of Isis-Fortuna. These are all presumably of Cypriote manufacture. Other Roman rings illustrated include one from Amathus with a plain sardonyx setting, of the second or third century AD, and a more flamboyant example, of third- or fourth-century date set with two sapphires.

Coins must be considered amongst the finer products of ancient artists, and it seems worthwhile to illustrate a few of Cypriote origin, or which were circulated in that island. Gold staters of Alexander were produced in several areas, and many bear much the same combination of Athena-head and Nike as does the example minted at Salamis in ill. 47. Again, Ptolemaic coins are somewhat monotonous in their use of a portrait head of the king and of an eagle on the reverse. Ill. 48 shows a high quality silver tetradrachm of Ptolemy v, minted at Kition in 174 BC. The two Roman bronze coins in ill. 49 may have been minted in Rome for distribution and use in Cyprus. One, a coin of Caracalla, shows the Temple of Aphrodite at Paphos; the other, of Vespasian, has a representation of Zeus Salaminios.

The arts and crafts of Hellenistic and Roman Cyprus are thus not as strongly Cypriote in appearance as were products of earlier times, being influenced by the wider artistic ambience of the powerful Hellenistic kingdoms, with their universal patronage of skilled men and artists, and by the continuing pressure of this atmosphere during the course of the Roman Empire. However, even here, Cyprus managed to make its own presence felt amongst many of the locally-made objects, and it is possible to use the term Cypriote art for products of the period between the reigns of Alexander and Constantine.

According to the New Testament (Acts XI, 19 and XIII, 4–13) Christianity was brought to Cyprus at an early date: first, by the Christians dispersed from Jerusalem by the persecution following the stoning of Stephen, and subsequently through the missionary activities of Paul and Barnabas in about AD 45. Barnabas in fact was a native of the city of Salamis, and was therefore bringing the new religion to his fellow-countrymen. How the Cypriote Church developed from then on is not well documented: a few funerary inscriptions hint at its presence in the second and third centuries, but firm evidence of its status only comes in the period after 312 when the Roman Emperor Constantine adopted Christianity and placed the Church throughout the Empire in a privileged position. Bishops from a number of Cypriote sees are recorded as attending important church councils from the Council of Nicaea in 325 onwards, and the archaeological evidence suggests that a major programme of church building began in the island, probably in the late fourth century.

In the face of attempts by the Patriarch of Antioch (in Syria) to assert his authority over the bishops of the island, particularly in the matter of the consecration of the Archbishop of Salamis, the Cypriote Church made out the case that by ancient tradition and because of its apostolic foundation it had always been independent of outside control. This 'autocephaly' of the Cypriote Church was accepted by the Council of Ephesus in 431 and was confirmed by the Emperor Zeno in 488.

The administrative history of Cyprus in the late Roman period is obscure, although we do know that from the end of the third century it formed part of the Diocese of the Orient, the head of which, later called the *comes Orientis*, was resident at Antioch. After severe earthquakes had shaken the island in the second quarter of the fourth century AD, it was Salamis, looking towards the Syrian coast, rebuilt and renamed Constantia in honour of Constantius II, which became the most important city and the seat of the governor, replacing the old capital at Nea Paphos. Administrative dependence on Antioch lasted until the reign of Justinian in the sixth century, when Cyprus was grouped with Caria, the Cyclades and two Danubian provinces, Scythia and Moesia Secunda, under the command of a military governor with the rank of *quaestor*. This extraordinary arrangement was soon criticised because of the inconvenience caused to provincials wanting to appeal to a governor stationed far away to the north near the Danube. An accommodation was reached whereby appeals could be heard instead at the imperial palace in Constantinople, though this must still have been far from ideal for the Cypriots. The reason for the grouping was doubtless a financial one: taxes from provinces such as Cyprus were probably intended to support increasingly expensive military operations against barbarians on the Danube frontier. The archaeological evidence certainly argues for the sixth and early seventh centuries having been a period of great prosperity in the island.

Since the early third century AD no coins had been struck in Cyprus. Its currency requirements had been met by imperial mints outside the island. Under Heraclius (in revolt 608–610, emperor 610–641),

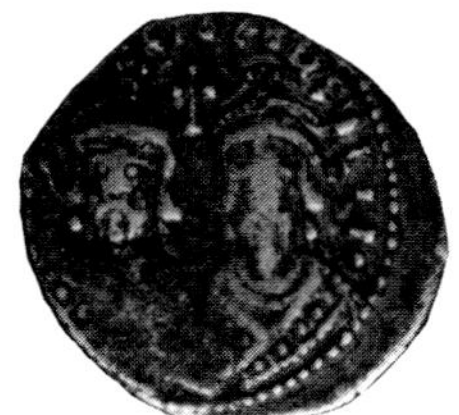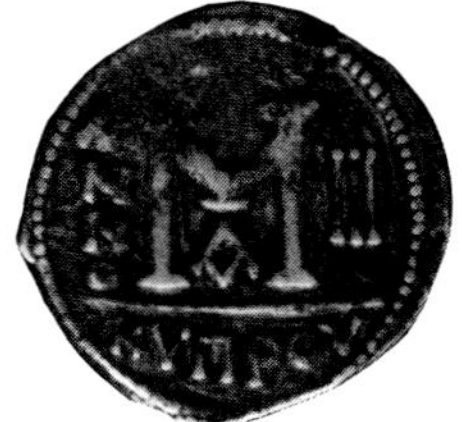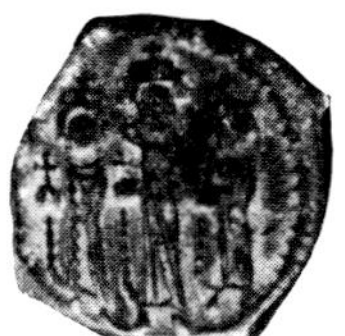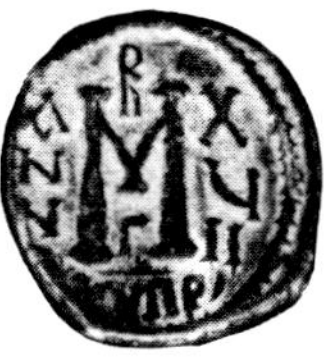

67 Bronze follis of Heraclius' revolt (in revolt
AD 608–10, emperor 610–641). 1970.7–5.3.

68 Bronze follis of Heraclius. AD 626/7. *BMC Heraclius* 269.

however, coinage was issued on two occasions, each of them in circumstances of crisis. The exact year of the earlier type (67) is as yet uncertain, but it belongs to a series issued by Heraclius and his father, the exarch of Africa (also called Heraclius) when in revolt against the Emperor Phocas. Heraclius and his father are depicted on the obverse of the coin (a bronze follis) wearing crowns and consular robes. On the reverse the letter M denotes the denomination. In the exergue is the Greek inscription KVΠPOV indicating a mint in Cyprus, in all likelihood situated at Salamis. In 610 Heraclius arrived in Constantinople and overthrew Phocas, but by this time the eastern provinces of the Empire had been for several years subject to attacks by the Sassanian Persians. These attacks increased in severity, culminating in 626 when the Persians in concert with the barbarian Avars besieged Constantinople itself. While the surrounding mainland provinces were overrun, Cyprus seems to have escaped, and in the years 626–628, coinage was again issued there. A bronze follis of the year 626/7 (68), smaller and lighter in weight than the earlier issue, shows on the obverse Heraclius flanked by his wife and son, and on the reverse in the exergue the inscription KVΠP.

By 628 the combined threat to the Empire had been defeated by vigorous military action, and Heraclius had even penetrated with his army deep into the Sassanian Empire. But considerable dislocation had been caused and when, within the space of two decades, a new enemy arose in the shape of the Arabs newly united under Islam, the exhausted empire was almost extinguished.

This time Cyprus did not remain immune. In 648/9 a strong Arab naval expedition, made up of contingents from newly conquered Syria and Egypt, attacked the island. Salamis was sacked and the rest of the island was plundered, although the expedition retreated when it was learnt that imperial reinforcements were approaching. A second expedition mounted in 653/4 again occupied Salamis and secured the surrender after a siege of another city, probably to be identified as Nea Paphos. A garrison was left behind to ensure that a yearly tribute was paid.

Towards the end of the nineteenth century a hoard of silver objects was found by local villagers in the ruins at the ancient site known as Lambousa, on the north coast a few miles to the west of Kyrenia. In 1902 a second much richer treasure was found at the same site. It seems likely that both of these treasures were buried for safety at the time of the Arab raids in the mid-seventh century.

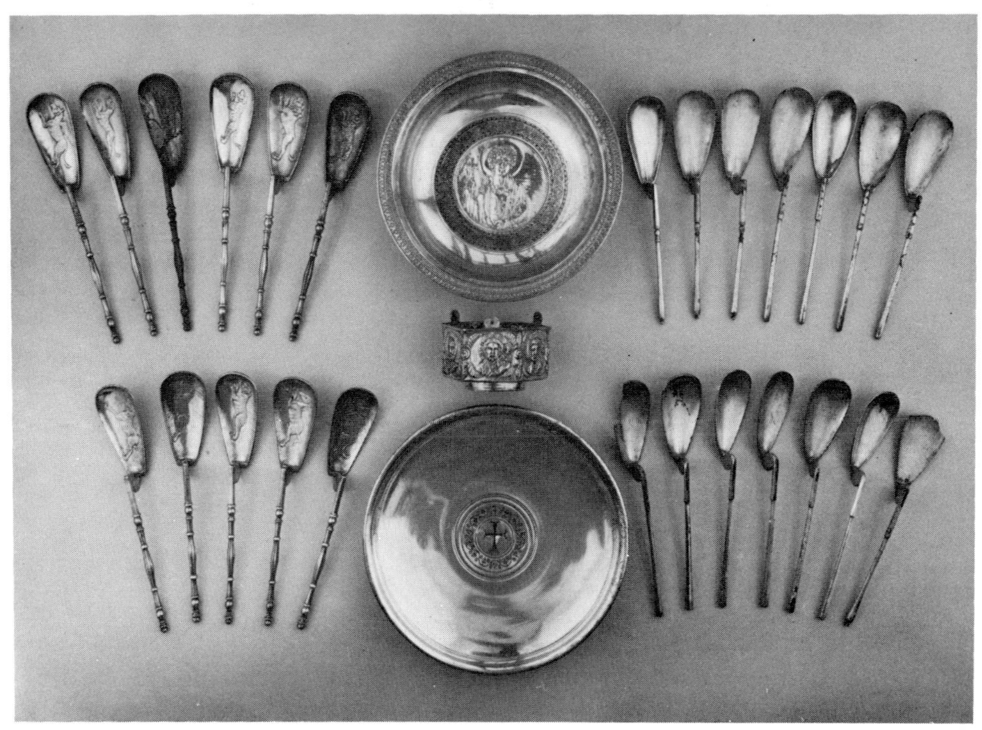

69 Deep bowl, hexagonal vessel, plate and spoons from the 'First Cyprus Treasure'. 1889.4–25.2, 3, 1, 4–28. D.24.7, 10.9, 27.1 cm, L.22.8–25.8 cm.

The 'First Cyprus Treasure' (69), which was purchased by the British Museum in 1899 after passing through various hands, consists of three vessels and twenty-five spoons. Since the three vessels seem to be of an ecclesiastical nature, it has been argued that the treasure must have belonged to a church. The flat dish or plate (69, bottom) is decorated with a cross in the centre surrounded by a circlet of ivy leaves inlaid with niello. It may well have served as a paten. In the bottom of the deep bowl (69, top) is depicted, within a circular band of nielloed ornament, the half-length figure of a military saint holding a cross in his right hand and wearing the uniform of an imperial guard, probably representing either St Sergius or St Bacchus. This could have been used as a basin for a priest to wash his hands in during the liturgy. The third vessel (69, centre and 70) could have served as a censer or as a hanging lamp. There were traces on the inside of a bronze lining, but no indication of a lid. Hexagonal in shape, it stands on a low circular foot and has three loops at the top for suspension. It is decorated in low relief on the sides with busts of Christ and the Virgin, each flanked by two saints. The twenty-five spoons belong to various types, representing survivals from at least four different sets. The most elaborate type, of which eleven survive, has a long baluster handle with a different wild animal or mythological beast depicted in the bowl of each. Such spoons may well have belonged to a church: gifts of spoons to churches in Western Europe in this period are recorded, but for what purpose is uncertain.

The second treasure, the bulk of which is now divided between the Metropolitan Museum in New York and the Cyprus Museum in Nicosia, was apparently found in two parts: a pot of gold jewellery

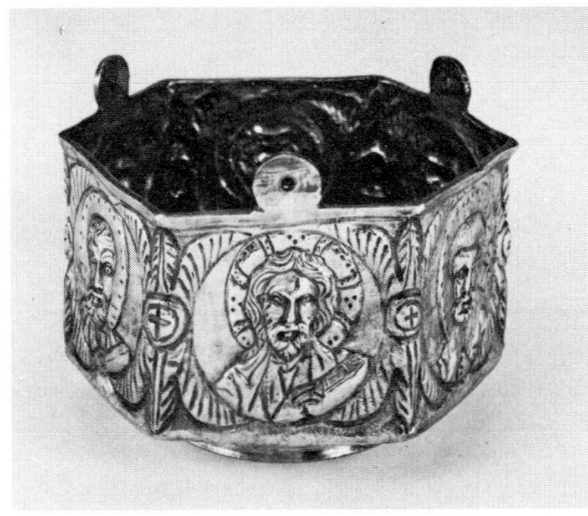

70 Hexagonal Vessel from the 'First Cyprus Treasure'. 1899.4–25.3.

71 Pair of gold earrings said to be from Lambousa. 1957.7–4.1, 2. H.3.5cm.

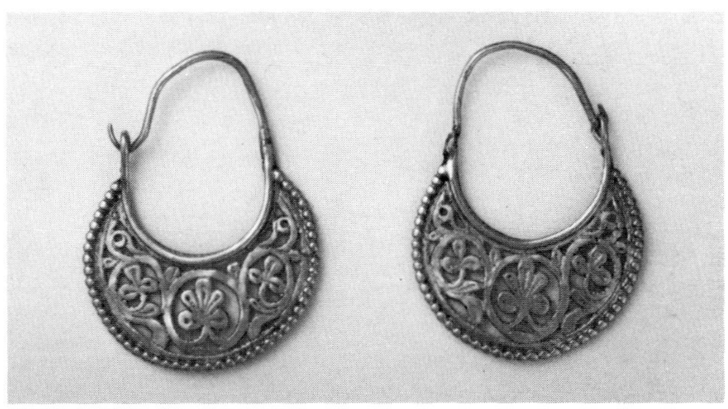

buried in the ground, and a number of silver plates hidden in a wall nearby. Of particular interest is a set of nine plates in three sizes each bearing a scene from the early life of King David, including his fight with Goliath, as recounted in the Old Testament. That these form an allegorical celebration of the Emperor Heraclius' victory over the Persians seems a convincing suggestion in the light of comparisons between Heraclius and David in contemporary literary sources.

Each of the silver vessels from the two treasures is stamped underneath with a set of control stamps of a type known from other silver objects of the period. There are normally five of these stamps in different shapes, and the dies seem to have belonged to a group of officials attached to the imperial court in Constantinople who supervised the stamping of silver objects as a guarantee of the quality of the silver. In many cases it can be seen that this was done before the objects received their final finish. Thus it is likely that the vessels from Lambousa were at least roughed out and probably also finished at Constantinople before being brought to Cyprus. The stamps provide clear evidence for dating since the bust and monogram of the reigning emperor appear on them, together with the names of the supervising officials, some of whom are known from other sources. Most of the vessels in the two treasures can be dated to the late sixth or early seventh century and the latest piece, the deep bowl with the military saint, is datable to the first decade of the reign of Constans II (641–651). The Arab raids of 648/9 and 653/4 therefore present the earliest likely occasion for the burial of the treasures by their owners.

Also said to be from Lambousa, and datable to the same period, is a

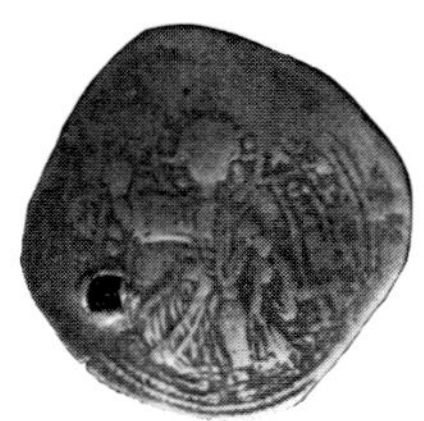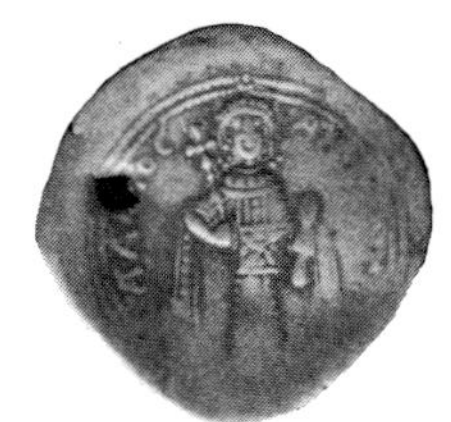

72 Billon *Trachy* of Isaac Comnenus, Usurper in Cyprus (1184–91). *BMC Isaac* II 32.

pair of gold ear-rings, now in the British Museum (71). The body of each is crescent-shaped with floral designs executed in open-work, suspended from a loop of gold wire at the top.

Cyprus now entered upon a period of three unhappy centuries for which the evidence is meagre and uncertain, but during which the island's fortunes clearly declined dramatically. At first under Arab domination, it was subsequently made into a kind of demilitarised 'no man's land' by agreement between the Arabs and what we should now call the Byzantine Empire, the continuation of the eastern part of the Roman Empire with its capital at Constantinople. This status seems to have persisted despite further Arab raids and occasional Byzantine attempts at reoccupation. Many villages and farms and even whole cities seem to have been abandoned in this period, though whether this was due more to the raids or to natural disasters such as drought and plague is unclear.

In 965 the island was reoccupied by the Byzantines on a more permanent basis, possibly in connection with major campaigns directed by the Emperor Nicephorus Phocas against the Arabs in Cilicia and Syria. Cyprus now remained in Byzantine hands for over two centuries, but not much is heard of the island until it acquired great strategic importance with the arrival of the Crusaders in the Holy Land at the end of the eleventh century. Thereafter, despite a number of severe raids from various quarters, it is apparent that recovery had set in. Castles were built, monasteries were founded and several churches still survive displaying frescoes painted in contemporary Constantinopolitan styles. The island was ruled by a series of governors drawn from the aristocracy of Constantinople and by this time Nicosia had emerged as their seat and capital.

This close Byzantine control was disrupted in 1184 when Isaac Comnenus, a member of the Byzantine imperial family, seized the island and proclaimed himself its emperor. As such he issued his own coinage, doubtless both for its value as propaganda and also to replace the supply normally received from Constantinople. Surviving examples of his coins include several types struck in the scyphate form (meaning cup-shaped), a shape of coin which had been introduced in the eleventh century in Byzantine coinage. The coin illustrated (72), shows on the obverse the enthroned Christ blessing, and on the reverse the standing figure of Isaac wearing imperial regalia.

Isaac did not enjoy his island empire for long. In 1191 the fleet of Richard Coeur-de-Lion, King of England, who was on his way to the Holy Land to take part in the Third Crusade, was dispersed by a storm and put into Limassol in disarray. Isaac tried to oppose the landing but was unsuccessful and Richard, realising the potential value of the island

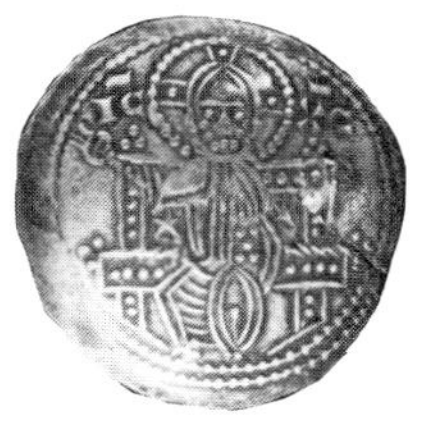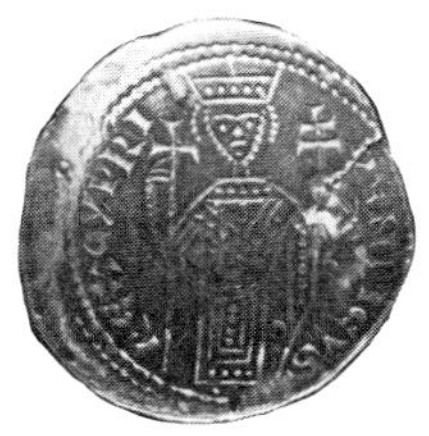

73 Base gold *Bezant* of Henry I de Lusignan (1218–53) 1925.1–5.186.

as a source of supply for the Crusade, decided to take possession of Isaac's 'empire' before continuing his journey to Palestine. After his departure the island proved troublesome to his deputies and he was also in need of ready cash. He therefore sold it, first to the Knights of the Order of the Temple, who also found it difficult to rule, and then in 1192 to the Latin King of Jerusalem, Guy de Lusignan, who had recently lost much of his kingdom to Saladin.

Under the Lusignan dynasty which ruled for the next three centuries, the social order of the island was radically altered. Guy adopted a policy of colonisation: Greek landlords were dispossessed and their lands granted as fiefs to followers of the Lusignans from the Latin Kingdom of Jerusalem and anyone else who could be attracted from the Crusader states. Although it continued to serve the bulk of the population, the Greek church was impoverished and moves were made in the 1220s to subject it to the Latin ecclesiastical hierarchy which had been set up in the island under the direction of the Papacy.

The Lusignans replaced the Byzantine coinage with a new currency inspired in part by the contemporary French system, although the highest denomination, the white (base gold) *bezant*, scyphate in form, was an imitation of the Byzantine gold coin, the *hyperpyron*. On an example struck by Henry I de Lusignan (73), the enthroned Christ is shown on the obverse, as with the type issued by Isaac Comnenus, with the king depicted in Byzantine imperial regalia on the reverse.

74 *Sgraffiato ware*
a) Bowl. H.8.4cm.
b) Goblet. H.12.5cm.
c) Bowl. H.12.1cm.
1895.8–10.8,1,3.

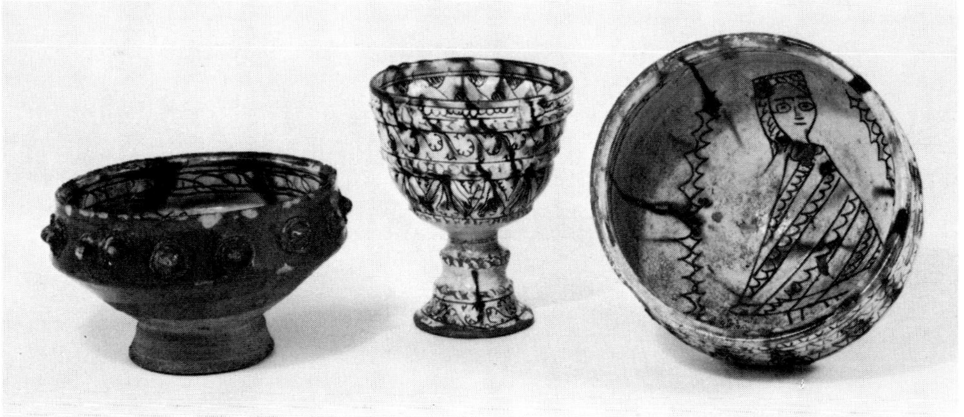

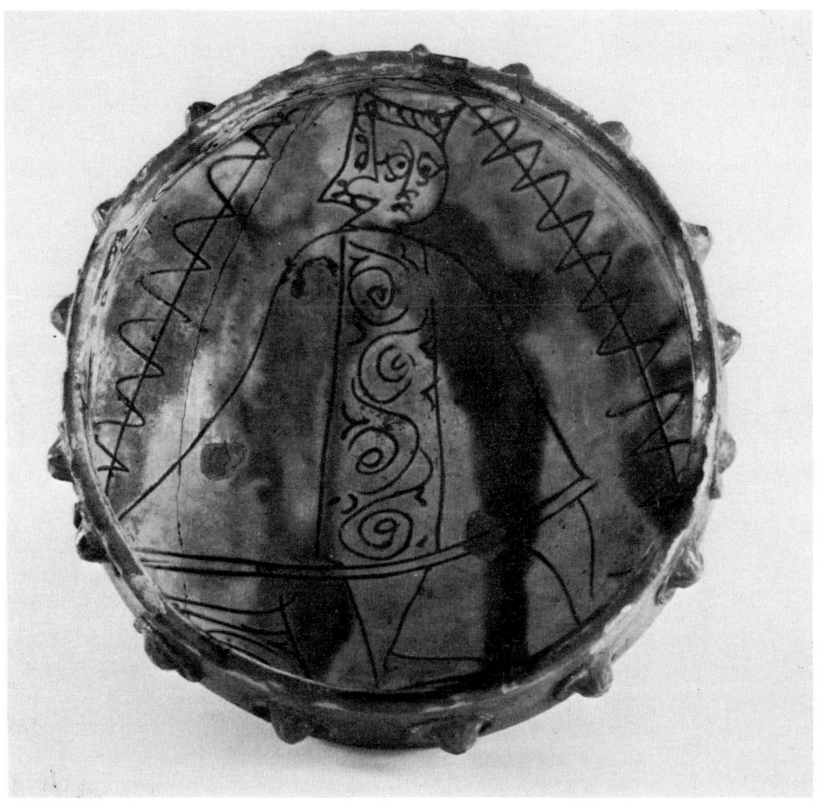

75 *Sgraffiato ware* bowl (view from above of bowl on left in 74) 1895.8–10.8.

Dating largely from the fourteenth and fifteenth centuries, is a kind of glazed pottery with characteristic *sgraffiato* decoration (from the Italian, meaning 'incised') (74, 75). Although the sites of the kilns where it was made are not yet known, it has been found frequently in the island and only rarely outside; it is therefore highly probable that it was manufactured locally.

It may have originated in the thirteenth century as an imitation of imported Byzantine plain-glazed *sgraffiato* pottery, but as it developed it seems to have been influenced by similar wares from Syria with colour-splashed glazes.

After an initial firing the pots were covered with a creamy-white slip (either on the inside alone or all over), through which designs and patterns were incised with a sharp point, revealing the darker clay beneath. A transparent glaze was then applied, dabbed or splashed with different metallic oxides, providing green and yellow-brown highlights of colour in the glaze. The pots then received a final firing stacked upside down on tripod spurs, which left visible scars in the glaze.

The commonest shapes amongst examples surviving complete are variants of a type of deep bowl with upturned rim standing on a circular foot (74, left), but goblets (74, centre), jugs and low dishes also occur. Beyond simple scribbles, the repertoire of incised designs includes geometric and floral motifs and animals, birds, and monsters. But perhaps the most attractive are the human figures which occur singly or as 'married' couples. Two examples are illustrated (74, right, and 75) which show male figures without arms, wearing rather shapeless cloaks or tunics and what are probably meant to be flat-topped caps on their heads.

Sherds are found in excavations of habitation sites, but curiously the vast majority of complete examples seems to have been found in graves in abandoned churchyards. Evidently it was a local custom for villagers to bury their dead with one or more of these pots and sometimes also with a coin. However, it seems likely that the ware was intended originally for use at the table and was not highly expensive. Certainly other wares were current in the period, including plain pottery for use in the kitchen. Poorer versions were still being made in the sixteenth century, but by this time the local market seems to have been flooded by imported North Italian *maiolica*.

During the thirteenth century Cyprus continued to be of great importance as a base for the defence of the beleaguered Crusader states. With their final demise in 1291, when Acre fell to the Egyptian Sultan, it remained a focus for Western European aspirations in the Near East and in fact gained an increased economic significance as one of the main centres for trade with Muslim lands. The port of Famagusta, the successor to Salamis (which had long been abandoned), became particularly wealthy, rivalling Alexandria and Constantinople itself as an entrepôt.

The Lusignan kings, however, did not enjoy control of this profitable trade. It was largely in the hands of the Italian merchants, chiefly citizens of the rival republics of Genoa and Venice, who did not remain for long content merely to trade. After an outbreak of hostilities in 1372 between the Genoese on the one side, and King Peter II on the other, the former obtained Famagusta as security for an indemnity imposed on the king. They managed to retain it until 1464. The Venetians also were no strangers to the practice of taking political control where once they had simply been merchants. They had long held an amorphous empire of ports and islands scattered through the Adriatic and Aegean seas. Under pressure in these areas from the Ottoman Empire, in 1489 they persuaded Caterina Cornaro, the Venetian widow of James the Bastard, the last Lusignan king, to abdicate in favour of the Republic of Venice. In her stead three rectors were appointed to rule the island, with their seat at Nicosia, together with a 'Captain of Cyprus' who was to act as commander-in-chief in peacetime, stationed at Famagusta.

The strong position Venice had acquired in Cyprus, leading to her acquisition of the island, had been brought about by sea power. In the sixteenth century her maritime supremacy was lost, and she fell back on a complicated system of diplomacy to maintain her position. The payment of tribute for the island which the Mameluke Sultans of Egypt had demanded since their successful raid on the island in 1426 was continued. After 1517 when the Mameluke dynasty was overthrown by the Ottoman Turks the tribute was paid instead to Constantinople, since 1453 the capital of the Ottoman Empire. Ottoman expansionism had become the chief danger to Venetian control. An invasion finally materialised in 1570, and the Venetians, despite the construction of excellent new fortifications particularly at Nicosia and Famagusta, found themselves overwhelmed by the size of the invading force. Nicosia fell after a month and the Turkish army moved on to invest Famagusta.

It was during the siege of Famagusta that copper coins with the nominal value of one *bezant* were struck to provide the hard-pressed authorities with funds to continue the defence (76). On the obverse is shown the Lion of St Mark, the ubiquitous symbol of the Republic, together with the legend PRO REGNI CYPRI PRESSIDIO ('for the garrison of the Kingdom of Cyprus') and the year – 1570. The inscription on the reverse referring to the 'inviolable promise of the Venetians' indicates the token nature of the issue.

After a siege of almost a year the city surrendered for lack of food and ammunition, the fleet which had been sent to relieve the island having failed to arrive. By the peace treaty concluded with the Sultan in 1573 Venice renounced all claim to Cyprus, which thus became part of the Ottoman Empire.

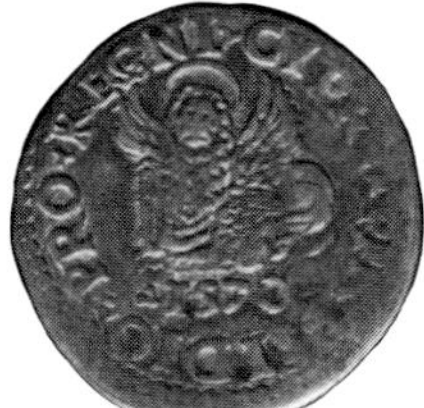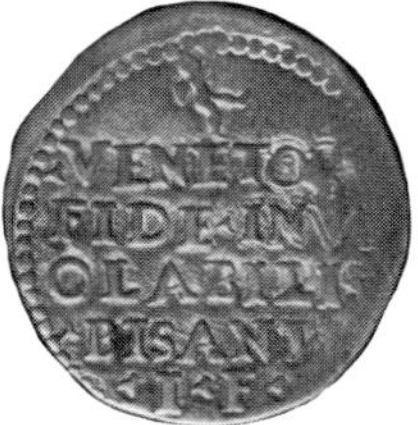

76 Venetian copper siege money of 1570 with the nominal value of one *Bezant*. 1870.5–7.8806.

Further reading

General

Art of Ancient Cyprus Museum of Fine Arts (Boston, 1972).

A. C. Brown and H. W. Catling, *Ancient Cyprus* (Ashmolean Museum, Oxford, 1975).

P. Dikaios, *A Guide to the Cyprus Museum* (3rd ed. Nicosia, 1961).

G. F. Hill, *A History of Cyprus*, 4 vols. (Cambridge, 1940–52).

V. Karageorghis, *The Ancient Civilisation of Cyprus* (London, 1969).

J. L. Myres, *Handbook of the Cesnola Collection, Metropolitan Museum of Art* (New York, 1914).

Current excavations are described annually by V. Karageorghis, '*Chronique des fouilles à Chypre*' in *Bulletin de Correspondance Hellénique* (Athens, since 1959).

Articles on Cypriote Archaeology are published in the annual *Report of the Department of Antiquities of Cyprus* (Nicosia).

For detailed discussions of material see the appropriate summary volumes of *The Swedish Cyprus Expedition* Vol. IV (Stockholm & Lund, 1948–72).

Neolithic to Bronze Age

J. M. Birmingham (ed.) *The Cypriot Bronze Age.* (Australian Studies in Archaeology 1 (1973), Sydney, 1974).

H. G. Buchholz & V. Karageorghis, *Prehistoric Greece and Cyprus: An Archaeological Handbook.* (London, 1973).

H. W. Catling, 'Cyprus in the Neolithic and Bronze Age Periods' in the *Cambridge Ancient History* (third edition, Cambridge, 1970–75) Vol. I Chapters IX (c) and XXVI (b); Vol. II Chapters IV (c) and XXII (b).

'Cyprus at the Dawn of her History'. *Archaeologia Viva* Vol. II. 3 (1969).

Geometric to Classical

V. Karageorghis and J. des Gagniers, *La Céramique Chypriote de Style Figuré* (Rome, 1974).

V. Karageorghis, *Kition* (London, 1976).

V. Karageorghis, *Salamis* (London, 1969).

Hellenistic and Roman

C. Vermeule, *Greek and Roman Cyprus* (Boston, 1976).

Medieval

E. C. Dodd, *Byzantine Silver Stamps* (Washington D.C., 1961).

A. and J. Stylianou, *The Treasures of Lambousa* (Nicosia, 1969).

British Museum Collection: Major Publications

D. M. Bailey, 'British Museum Excavations at Hala Sultan Tekke in 1897 and 1898: The Material in the British Museum' in P. Aström et al., *Hala Sultan Tekke* 1 (Studies in Mediterranean Archaeology XLV.1, Gothenburg, 1976).

D. M. Bailey, *Catalogue of the Lamps in the British Museum*, Vol. 1 (London, 1975).

V. E. G. Kenna, *Catalogue of the Cypriote Seals of the Bronze Age in the British Museum: Corpus of Cypriote Antiquities 3.* (Studies in Mediterranean Archaeology xx.3, Gothenburg, 1971).

F. H. Marshall, *Catalogue of the Finger-Rings, Greek, Etruscan and Roman in the Departments of Antiquities, British Museum.* (British Museum, London, 1907; reprinted 1968).

F. H. Marshall, *Catalogue of the Jewellery, Greek, Etruscan and Roman in the Departments of Antiquities, British Museum.* (British Museum, London, 1911; reprinted 1969).

A. S. Murray, A. H. Smith, H. B. Walters, *Excavations in Cyprus* (British Museum, London, 1900; reprinted 1970).

F. N. Pryce, *Catalogue of Sculpture in the Department of Greek and Roman Antiquities, British Museum.* Vol. 1, part 2 (London, 1931).

A. H. Smith, *Corpus Vasorum Antiquorum: Great Britain I: British Museum 1.* (British Museum, London, 1925).

H. B. Walters, *Catalogue of the Greek and Etruscan Vases in the British Museum,* Vol. 1 part 2 (British Museum, London, 1912).

H. B. Walters, *Catalogue of the Terracottas in the Department of Greek and Roman Antiquities, British Museum* (London, 1903).